Just Married!

Marital Bliss with 8 Simple Marriage Habits for Healthy Intimacy and a Mindful Relationship

Marvin Mills

from various sources. Please consult a licensed professional before attempting any techniques outlined in this book.

By reading this document, the reader agrees that under no circumstances is the author responsible for any losses, direct or indirect, that are incurred as a result of the use of the information contained within this document, including, but not limited to, errors, omissions, or inaccuracies.

Table of Contents

YOUR FREE GIFT

As a way of saying thank you for your purchase, I am pointing you to 2 videos on the subject of **marriage** and the **differences between men and women**. Both videos are hilarious. Hope you enjoy them!

The 1st video is from American speaker and author Jenna McCarthy who writes about relationships, marriage and parenting. She shares surprising research on how marriages (especially happy marriages) really work in her own entertaining way.

The 2nd video brings you the insight of John Gray, American relationship counselor, lecturer and author of the world famous 1992 book "Men Are From Mars, Women Are From Venus". In his inimitable way, almost as a stand-up comedian, he presents his view on the differences between men and women.

>> To get your video links, please visit <<

https://bit.ly/3bmiLHf

Introduction

"We come to love not by finding the perfect person, but by learning to see an imperfect person perfectly."

—Sam Keen

The plane has landed, and you two are officially done with the honeymoon. The days before the wedding have been tiring, and the extensive itinerary just added more to the fatigue. You arrive at your new place, hand in hand, and before entering, look at each other with hope and love—and the promise that this new adventure together is going to be better than any experience you two have had before.

The majority of the movies we see end here. The couple gets married and drives off for their honeymoon in complete bliss. But what happens after the honeymoon? What happens when the couple finally starts to live together? There is a reason why they don't show you that in movies. We, on the other hand, will. Maybe we can't show you, but we'll surely leave you with some great visions and images—some of which will make you laugh hysterically and some that will get you right in the feels.

All in all, if you have decided to give this a read, let's begin.

According to Dr. Ted Huston, a professor at the University of Texas, Austin, the first two years of marriage are the most crucial for couples. They are also the best predictor of stressors and marital satisfaction—something that nearly all couples experience, new or old. In one study, he interviewed many newlyweds and discovered that the first two years of marriage, as happy as they may seem, also sees the worst of both partners. There is an abatement of love, an increase in ambivalence, unresponsiveness from partners and a decline in overt affection. He suggests that there is only one formula to determine if the couple will last forever or become unhappily-ever-after, and that involves noticing the difference that is apparent right after the knot has been tied.

To prove his hypothesis, he gathered 156 couples married in 1981. He tracked their marital status, expanded family, social status, general livelihood over the course of the next thirteen years. Out of those 156 couples:

- Sixty-eight were happily married
- Thirty-two were unhappily married (but still together)
- And fifty-six divorced

The couples that divorced during the first two years after their marriage depicted signs of disillusionment and negative feelings toward each other in the first few months. He explained how many couples are often disillusioned when starting their marital life. They consider marriage a bed of roses, but soon they discover they have to deal with the thorns, too. The couples who were happily married even after thirteen years had positive feelings about their spouses during the first few months and overlooked or worked together to resolve issues and meet each other's expectations.

The couples who divorced within the first two years showed signs of disillusionment and were negative toward one another. (Feuerman, 2020).

This is why many still believe that reaching the first-year mark as a happily married couple is, in itself, a remarkable milestone. If we look at modern marriage, we see even more complications than before. Previously, women rarely saw that window of freedom and divorce open to them. It was something looked down upon and rather discouraged. So they spent on living their lives miserably with men who didn't respect them or love them. But it wasn't just women who suffered. Their counterparts did, too. Men dealt with their fair share of demanding and challenging women who were disinterested in them and only living with them because they had to. Divorce for men was also thought of as something too extreme and they were often advised to bend their wives into submission instead of divorcing them.

Though modern marriage may not see similar challenges, it does have to deal with a number of them to keep the marriage blissful and happy. You have spent the last year or two imagining how it would be, put your heart and soul into the wedding planning, but now, suddenly, it's all over. You realize you've spent way too much on the wedding and are already discussing how you two will manage the finances moving forward. Then, you also have your respective careers to think of, each more demanding than the other. You are worried if your job will become a problem with all the house chores that need to be taken care of… but these are just some basics.

According to relationship therapist Aimee Hartstein, the first year is the hardest for couples—all jokes aside. This is true even for couples who have spent years living together. The start of married life is tricky. Period. Some small part of the challenge has to do with the stress of the months leading up to the marriage. Many couples, despite having a stringent budget, have a tendency to overspend. Accommodating guests' requests for a last-minute plus one, changes in the menu, floral arrangements need more work, etc. are all very real issues to deal with.

Another rather debatable reason is that marriage is different from being in cohabitation. The biggest difference between the two is that when you're just living together, you still have the option to walk out the door and never return. With marriage, things get a bit more complicated, and these negative feelings only seem to deepen as the divorce proceedings start. The couple is asked to highlight each other's negative attributes, there is character assassination, and both leave the meeting feeling stupid and confused (Did I really fall for that person?) Marriage is a permanent union and every fight or argument that the couple has feels more significant than before—because it is. Before marriage, every fight seemed workable and if it didn't, you two spent some time apart and to yourself to figure stuff out. With marriage, you don't have that leverage—everything has to be discussed mutually, and you start to see every fight as this-is-how-it-is-going-to-be-for-the-rest-of-my-life.

And again, that is just another basic—we haven't even gotten to the in-laws bit.

Then comes the legal aspect of things, such as how to manage finances, who will pool in how much, who will be responsible for the groceries, bills, and savings. New couples often squabble over such practicalities in the first month of marriage. Then, there is updating passport, licenses, deciding whether or not to get a joint account, and writing thank-you cards.

In a survey of 75,000 married couples by Lastling, a health app, couples that yearn for domestic bliss mostly end up fighting about domestic chores. Who does the dishes and who puts the trash out might not seem big enough reasons for arguments, but when you keep having the same argument every single night, it leaves behind some unpleasant feelings.

Another thing that often gets neglected is how the couple spends their free time. Picture this: your idea of spending free time is to just chill on a couch and catch up on sports, whereas hers includes getting into a bubble bath or watching something together on Netflix.

Right here is a conflict of ideas, and although sometimes couples do come to a mutual understanding, it can cause a rift when they don't. Another scenario would be the man wanting to go out with his friends to the bar, but the wife wants the spouse to stay at home with them. When either of the spouses is denied their guilty pleasures and have to compromise to reach a mutual ground, one can expect some spats.

And finally, there is a difference in opinions and expectations. The things that previously attracted the partners to each other, such as physical attraction, personality connections, common interests, and sexual passion, become less central as the realities of life set in. They have to settle for what "we" want as opposed to what "I" want. A common example of this would look something like this: one partner demanding more intimacy, while the other doesn't seem in the mood for it. Again, another cause for a fight.

But do you know the best part? There is only one problem causing all these issues in the first place—and the problem is the solution, too! Confused? Let me explain.

Communication!

Poor communication—be it about one's likes, interests, or expectations—is the root cause. Couples who don't talk or openly express their opinions and feelings suffer the most. Take any relationship—the relationship between a boss and an employee, a child and its mother, a teacher and their pupils, the foundation of every relationship is built on how effective the communication is between the two. You can't expect a boss to not tell the employee what is wanted of him, you can't expect a mother to not pay attention to her little one, and you certainly can't expect a teacher to instill values and morals in her students without proper communication and guidance.

YourTango.com, a lifestyle website, conducted a national poll of 100 mental health specialists and concluded that poor communication was indeed cited as the most common issue among couples and also the one that leads to divorce followed by the inability of spouses to resolve conflicts (Bilow, 2013). Furthermore, the poll also revealed that men and women had different communication complaints. Men, seventy percent of them, cited nagging and constant complaining as the foremost communication problem whereas eighty-three percent of women cited lack of validation of their feelings or opinions by their spouses as the biggest communication problem.

But long before these findings were determined, many marriage counselors and therapists had already hinted the same. Take John Gottman and Gary Chapman, for example. John Gottman has over 40 years of experience helping couples find their way back to each other and resolve issues that once seemed the final straw in their marriage. To him, there are four main types of communication problems that often take couples down the divorce lane (Gottman, n.d.). These include:

1. Stonewalling (Giving your partner the cold shoulder and becoming emotionally withdrawn)
2. Criticism of the partner's personality (Wanting to change things about the partners and constantly nagging them when they repeat the same behaviors)
3. Contempt (Using statements that stem from a relative stance of superiority)
4. Defensiveness (Not being able to take criticism and getting riled up over every little detail)

But hopefully, you will never have to worry about that—we are going to make sure that the first year of your marriage, and the second and the third, are all as delightful as possible. Together, we shall look at all those factors that play a crucial role in how couples communicate and live in harmony, and develop eight such habits that will make their marriage a success—something they will be discussing with their kids and grandkids later on.

This book holds the answers you have been seeking when it comes to surviving the first year of marriage. It is for every future wife or husband-to-be, and also for those who have just said their vows and are wondering how to begin their new lives together. *Just Married* shares relatable tips, suggestions, and ideas for overcoming everyday married life struggles to enjoy harmony, happiness, and mutual respect. But before we make the first 365 days of togetherness harmonious and full of love, let me introduce myself and let you know why you should listen to what I have to say.

Hi, I'm Marvin Mills. I am an author who has always had an avid interest in personal development. I firmly believe in the incredible potential of people to shape their lives and become the most successful they can be.

Eager to share with others the knowledge that I have accumulated, I started a writing journey. I write on the topics of self-improvement, healthy habits, and relationship strategies to experience romantic bliss.

All of my work is based on my education and the experience I've gathered through the years. I obtained my undergraduate degree in applied psychology and a master's degree in criminology. Through my personal experience in working with young people from dysfunctional families, starting several businesses, working in HR, and much more, I embrace the value of self-control and aim to help readers explore their limits and expand their potential on the road to a better life.

I am an animal lover and enjoy long walks with my two Rhodesian Ridgebacks, Reece and Nalu.

Chapter 1:

The Honeymoon Is Over—

Now What?

When we fall in love for the first time, we can't help but be smitten. Everything about our lover finds a way to our hearts. Their smile, love-filled glance, touch, compliments... it all makes us wonder if life can be more beautiful than this.

The first few days or weeks after the marriage are quite an apt definition of the honeymoon phase. Recently married couples go on a romantic getaway to be closer and more intimate with one another. Love and laughter are addictive. It is hard to keep our hands to ourselves, and no matter how much time you spend with them, the fear of being apart is nerve-wracking. You vow to never let go of each other's warm and comfy embrace and promise to always wake up with smiles on your faces. Every thought in your mind surrounds them, every vision you have of your future includes them with you. You easily brush off any inconvenient issues, like placing the wet towel on the bed or not changing socks for three days straight, because life has so much more to offer and you want to make every second of your time together count. You put in the extra effort to look your best, seduce them with your sexual moves, be patient with them, and keep reminding yourself that this is perhaps the best decision of your life. Many couple therapists believe that it is the hormones doing all the thinking here. The reason we are willing to overlook inconveniences is that we subconsciously think that they don't matter and will, with time, change.

And then, one day, it happens.

Okay, maybe not in just a day, but you see where I'm going with this. You wake up next to them and no longer feel the butterflies in your stomach. Your rose-colored glasses are off and you begin to look at them for who they are, not what they represent. Their charms are no longer working, the sex has become almost non-existent, and although you still love hanging out with them, you can do with some time away from them, too. No need to panic if you are going through the same. It isn't the end of the world—or your relationship—but rather just the end of the honeymoon phase. Here are some more signs to really know when it is happening or worse, has already happened.

Sign #1: You Seem Bored

Things that once seemed exciting no longer do. You often debate about what to watch on the weekends, don't want to get all dressed up, the lovey-dovey texts are no longer consistent, kissing has reduced to a minimum, and you can never decide on anything to do together and prefer spending some time alone or with your individual friends. The reason to discuss this as the first sign is that often couples mistake it for consistency and routine. They assume that all relationships take this turn after some time, but this isn't true. Some couples wait for their partners to get home and can't wait to kiss them like it's the first time. Some couples fight each other to spend more time together. Some couples text each other about every small and big highlight of the day, from what they ate or who they saw walking down the street from their office window. If the euphoria and excitement seem to be missing, then it likely means you are bored with each other.

Sign #2: Foreplay Time Has Decreased and Sex Has Become Mechanic

When the marriage is fairly new or you two have recently moved in together, there is a thrill to exploring each other's bodies. Each partner is only learning to establish their preferences and guiding each other in this regard. This can be both fun and exciting, as there is so much you can try to keep the relationship alive. The passionate sessions are longer and steamier. It all usually begins with anticipation, followed by a ton of foreplay. Foreplay plays a critical role in setting the mood and getting both partners aroused for the finale or showdown.

But now that the honeymoon period is over, you can't avoid noting the lack of this excitement. Sometimes, there isn't any foreplay and sex seems like a ritual that you have to perform to reassure yourself that things haven't changed. But they have, and you know it in your heart. Rarely do you feel the kind of passion that turns you on so much that you can't wait to get your hands on your spouse. Sex is quick, with mechanical, routine moves. There are fewer emotions involved and usually one or both partners are left unsatisfied. This change in our attitudes and expectations with sexual intimacy is driven by a stable kind of libido, rather than by infatuation or lust. You begin to seek familiarity and routine. Maybe it is because you think that there is little to explore further, but trust me when I tell you this, if you are looking for means to spice up the sex, you are already in a deep rut.

Sign #3: You Become Easily Annoyed

Previously, you were able to overlook minor irritations in their behaviors and actions, but you no longer can. As the honeymoon phase passes, you begin to shove that extra patience you previously had in a drawer and begin to scrutinize everything about them with your glasses on. Every little thing they do annoys you and you feel like a boiling pressure cooker, just waiting to burst. Things you were able to ignore before no longer seem small and you find yourself pulling up your sleeves, ready for conflict.

For example, picture this: you're watching your favorite sports team play against last year's champions. It's a crucial match that your team just has to win to get ahead on the points table. It's the final few minutes before the game ends, and your wife picks up the phone and calls up her best friend. She is laughing, talking about routine stuff, and being herself, but what she doesn't know is how annoying her voice seems at the moment. You just want to concentrate on the game peacefully, and she can't even give you that. Suddenly, your mind starts to wander and you begin to mentally count all the times she has done this, becoming suspicious that she does it on purpose to annoy you.

Irritation is bound to build up in your system, and even though it is just a little thing, it annoys the very core of you. Instead of politely asking her to take her conversation into another room so that you can watch the game in some peace and quiet, you lash out. You throw the remote, shout at her for being so loud, and leave the room, slamming the door behind you.

You are unable to think clearly or differentiate between a coincidence and a deliberate attempt to piss you off.

Sign #4: Communication Feels Like an Obligation

This isn't necessarily true for all couples, especially those who turned from friends to lovers, but communication at times can feel like something you just have to do. There are times in a marriage where one partner wants to discuss every minor thing with their spouse while the other doesn't really get the point of the discussion. Yet, they still have to lend their ears and act like they care, because they don't want to hurt their partner's feelings. However, this can become harder to do every passing day, and more challenging to keep up with.

On the other hand, some partners constantly demand validation of their opinions and think that communication is the best way to go about it. What they fail to realize is that their constant need for approval and validation can seem like nagging.

"You never ask for my opinion about things. You always decide for yourself without considering my feelings. You are so selfish!"

"You don't have to ask for permission about every little thing."

When this becomes the norm, you know the good times are past you. Couples should never feel burdened to do something.

Sign #5: You Disagree More

There are more conflicts than before as you can't seem to compromise over things like you used to. Quite frankly, couples stop agreeing to things mutually as their ego doesn't allow them to bend to their partner's demands. Even when you try your hardest not to sound too harsh, unpleasant, or demanding, you somehow end up coming across that way. It isn't like you don't want to respect your partner's opinions or appear closed-minded, but you do. Earlier, for the sake of their love and so as not to appear too childish, you agreed to things in an effort to impress them and come off as caring and devoted. But just because you have said no to something for the first time doesn't mean the end of the honeymoon phase. It just shows you aren't willing to blindly agree with everything they say or do. Maybe it's just your way of setting some boundaries early on.

For example, if one partner is in the mood for intimacy but the other one isn't and says no, it doesn't mean they will never be together again. Many more factors, such as tiredness, tough days at work, or sleep deprivation, can be to blame. Mostly, couples find a way around it and learn to discuss such things before requesting them and consider each other's wishes.

Sign #6: There Are No Butterflies in Your Stomach

Or in the air, for that matter. Everything seems a bit dull and routine. You don't get that feeling of nervousness when you lay eyes on them after they return from work. It doesn't mean that you aren't happy to see them, it just doesn't leave you with the same excitement anymore. Remember the days when you two were dating and they sent you a text that they were just around the corner, ready to pick you up for dinner? Remember how jittery and nervous you felt with happiness? You were so concerned about how you looked, whether the makeup was too much, the dress too provocative, what you would talk about, what would happen after dinner? All these thoughts and more went through your head when you were dating. But now, the only thoughts you will have are if they've brought back the groceries you asked for, have they paid the bill on their way home, etc. In simpler terms, you don't get those butterflies in your tummy anymore.

Sign #7: You Get on Each Other's Nerves More

When we are in the honeymoon phase, we get to know our partner's personality, but it is only when we start to live with them and realize there is no escaping that we begin to notice how flawed they are. But they were never perfect in the first place—it is only your perception changing over time. You begin to point each other's imperfections out loud and it starts to get on your nerves.

"You shouldn't have married me in the first place if you found me this annoying!"

"I wish I had known earlier how unhygienic you are. You haven't taken a bath in like three days, Mark."

"God, I don't know how much longer I can take this nagging from you, Julie. You're testing my patience now."

These are just examples of what marriage after the honeymoon phase looks like, but don't lose hope yet. There is a silver lining to the life-after-honeymoon, too.

So Is It the End of Us?

Well, hold your horses there, young couple! We never said that. Maybe I did scare you a little by beginning the book on a negative note, but things are only going to get better from here on. As per Louis de Bernières, when someone falls in love, it's a bit like temporary madness. Being a best-selling author of his time, he did know a few insights on what love feels and looks like. Although there were no cellphones or message services in his time, we can't really apply his wisdom to the love of today. Yet, he still manages to grasp the core idea of what love feels like during the start of any relationship. In his book, written during the time of World War II, he summed up some significant aspects of the honeymoon period which included fluffy-headedness, neglectful attitude towards work, and abandonment of social life. However, when couples move past this stage, they don't stop loving each other but rather evolve together to have an even deeper connection than before. Lust is turned into love and partnership is turned into companionship.

Couples aim for a more relaxed approach toward their partner and begin to accept them for who they are. The things that annoyed them right after the honeymoon phase ended become workable. Couples find their rhythm and find a way to avoid conflicts and arguments. So, to think that the loss of the honeymoon phase is entirely a bad thing is wrong. There's so much good that comes from it, and once you are done reading the described changes, you will notice that the positives win over the negatives.

So, let's see if you have a chance of developing true love or not.

You Are Less Freaked Out About Little Bumps Along the Way

Take any new relationship, be it between partners or friends, and you'll see that a lot of uncertainty and insecurity revolves around the budding relationship.

The expectations are too high and the chances of fights breaking out are more. But once you have passed that phase of uncertainty and come to completely trust each other to handle anything life throws at you, you become less anxious about what's to come. You don't lose your mind or start to panic when you foresee financial problems. You know that you will make it through, despite the inconsistencies and unpredictability. You also learn to get over fights quicker than before, and begin to view arguments as something rather temporary. It is pleasant to have that kind of trust and security in the relationship, which is only possible once the couple has passed the honeymoon phase.

You Are Less Intimidated by Each Other's Families

Meeting the parents for the first time—can there be anything more daunting than that? But once the initial meetings with parents and extended family are done with, it becomes easier for partners to relax around each other's families and feel like home. They no longer intimidate you and you don't feel judged over your choice for a spouse. (*Although, let's be honest, some parents who are overly possessive about their kids may demean you at some point, but that doesn't mean they disapprove of you.*)

You Develop a Comfortable Routine

With time, couples learn to develop routines and schedules that suit their customized needs. For instance, if one or both partners go to work, or one works from home and the other goes to the office, they find a balance between their individual lives and make time for each other when together. They also decide on whose family to visit for dinner over the weekend and how to spend their free time. Simply put, there is less spontaneity and more consistency. There is a predictability that only happens when the honeymoon phase is over.

Together, You Can be More Vulnerable

During the honeymoon phase, couples often hide their true feelings about things because they want to please the other person. They want to be thought of as caring and loving and often "pretend" to act a certain way to keep their partners interested in them. But once they make it past that phase, they become more open and concerned about each other's opinions and feelings. They begin to value their partners more, with greater understanding. There is no masking of emotions involved. They can be vulnerable without fear and expect their partners to understand what they are going through. This often involves crying or throwing a temper tantrum in front of them without a care in the world because, at the end of the day, they both know that it's okay to express feelings and emotions as they are together for the long haul. Since there is more openness in the relationship, support also increases and both partners feel less embarrassed about how they feel and voice out their concerns more confidently.

You Care Less About Each Other's Appearance

Once the relationship has passed a certain phase, partners become more comfortable around each other. They no longer care if you have no makeup on or look dressed up for a night out. They'll be okay with taking you places in a sweatshirt and messy bun. The same applies to women. They stop expecting their partners to dress to the nines at all times. Besides, you two have seen each other in rather very compromising positions, so it doesn't matter if you look perfect. Many women also report feeling less pressure to wax or shave and get all dolled up. At this point, the relationship is less reliant on how a person looks and more on how they make you feel when you are around them. It is more about their personality and not their looks. The attraction becomes attachment and care.

You Act More Real

During the honeymoon phase, couples act all lovey-dovey and put themselves out a lot more. There is extra makeup, sexy dressing, sexier lingerie, steamy intimacy, and lots of pretending. They want the other partner to like them and not think that they have made a mistake in marrying them. So, they will deliberately appear more likable so that the other person accepts them. This kind of thinking also stems from fear of not being good enough, as one or both the partners are unsure of themselves. But once that phase is over, couples start to shed their layers and show their partners who they really are. It isn't as bad as it sounds, but rather a positive thing as it makes room for a deeper connection and a stronger bond. The big reveal also pulls the curtain from some flaws but there is always room for improvement and enhancement.

You Learn to Say and Hear 'No'

As it is no longer a race to impress or get along, couples will learn to say no to their partners and accept it when being told. This doesn't mean that disagreements increase, it just means more understanding is established between them where they start to value their partner's opinions and suggestions more. It is also a sign that they become more honest with each other and are okay with receiving honesty in return without a conflict.

You Learn to Handle Disagreements

Disagreements are a natural thing to happen when two people are involved. Even if they are exact copies of each other—i.e., have the same passions and interests—they are still bound to find one another in the middle of an argument. However, when the honeymoon phase is over, they become more mature about handling conflicts and learn to move past them. They both know that they are in this together forever and thus have the resolve to quickly get over things that cause a rift between them. Even if that means engaging in more than a dozen fights during a week, they still find ways to resolve it and reach a middle ground where neither of them feels left out or degraded. This is a clear sign of progression in the relationship.

You Don't Hold Back Your Emotions

If one partner feels like crying, they can do so without being judged—and that also includes ugly crying where your nose is dripping and you make abnormal sounds. This is only possible when the couple has passed that stage where they feel uncomfortable being so relaxed around each other. Instead, the partner usually grabs a tissue and wipes your nose and tears and holds you closer until you stop crying.

You Know the Love is Real

You've been with each other for enough time now that you've seen them at their worst. If that didn't make you leave them, there is little chance that you will later on. You have seen them throw tantrums, you have seen how they act like a sloth on a Sunday and you have accepted their habits like not putting the seat of the toilet down, leaving wet hair in the drain, farting, snoring... I could go on with this list, but you get the point, right?

You've accepted them for who they are and have stopped trying to change them. This is what real love looks like. You are happy with what they have to offer and you work around their flaws without making them feel bad. In short, she puts the toilet seat down and you clean the drain. This shows that you two are in it for the long run.

You Get Over the Peachiness of Things

Life gets back to normal again once the celebratory phase has passed. When it comes to discussing with others how well or not-so-well your marriage is going, you don't only focus on the good things. You mention the not-so-cute stuff about your partner, too. You openly admit that it is more than just hugs, cuddles, and kisses. You don't care what the other person might think about it, but you know in your heart that it doesn't matter. You two feel stable and committed in your relationships—with or without the cutesy stuff.

You Are Okay With Not Feeling Well

Or perhaps you are comfortable telling them about it without feeling awkward. Imagine this: you had your get together with the guys and ate more-than-you-can-handle tacos and Mexican chili tortillas. You come home with an upset tummy and know all hell is about to break loose. You don't keep that stuff from them, but instead mentally prepare them for what's to come—loud farts and multiple visits to the bathroom. Now imagine, had this been the honeymoon phase, would you have felt this comfortable sharing it with them and expecting them to be completely okay with it? Probably not!

Conversely, if your partner is having bad period cramps, she doesn't give you the silent treatment or ask you to leave her alone. No, she asks you to bring some ice-cream and turn on some hot water in the bathtub for a relaxing bath. Earlier, she might have canceled a date and lied about having the flu, but not anymore. This kind of comfort is only achievable once you are out of the lovey-dovey phase.

You Talk Comfortably About Childhood and Relatives

We all have people in our families that we wish we could hide from everyone, especially our significant other. There are also some past traumas that we may not feel comfortable sharing with our spouses until we have been together for a while. And don't even get me started on ex-partners.

During the honeymoon phase, it all seems too soon to share such intimate and private details about yourself and your family, but the minute you do, know that you have successfully made it past the honeymoon phase and are still closer than ever. You no longer carry the burdens alone and don't feel judged when sharing such details with your partner.

You Both Know Your Boundaries Well

From the minute partners decide to be in a relationship, they establish some unsaid boundaries between them. These usually include things like no cheating, giving them more of your free time, being honest with them, being more invested in their likes and interests, etc. Once their relationship reaches the stage of maturity, i.e. past the honeymoon phase, these boundaries become clearer and stronger. Both partners understand that they have to comply with some rules at all times, now that they are in holy matrimony. Many couples assume that boundaries are bad, but they aren't. Boundaries are essential for healthy relationships and allow couples to trust each other with more compassion, and avoid doing things they aren't comfortable with.

Emotional Connection Strengthens Between You

You may not be rolling under the sheets as often, but you will surely develop a much stronger and deeper bond that doesn't involve having sex all the time. It's hard for couples in the honeymoon phase to imagine how they will ever be able to keep their hands off of each other, but when they do, it doesn't necessarily mean the end of them. The slowing down of hormones and the increased familiarity with bodies makes more room for emotional stability and intimacy. You may still have sex every single night, but it is no longer just about that. You can also spend nights without it and just lay in bed and talk with each other. Trust me, sometimes, this is more satisfying than a few minutes of physical intimacy.

Remember when we told you that the pros of passing the honeymoon phase outweigh the cons? Well, here you have it. Not to mention, the stronger your bond becomes, the more comfortable you two feel with each other. Your communication becomes better and more meaningful. You are willing to let go of a few nips and slips in their actions, like their laziness to do the cleaning or get the car fixed. You are willing to accept them for who they are, with all their imperfections, and learn to live with them. You establish healthy boundaries and work through your differences in a calm and composed manner. There are fights, but these are only temporary, and you work them out sooner than before. And, most importantly, you learn to listen and apologize for your shortcomings and misjudgments. There is a little element of name-and-shame, as you two are well aware of the fact that it is now up to you two to either make the relationship work or let it go sour.

Now that we have learned what the first year looks like, more or less, it's time to move onto developing some healthy habits to ensure the relationship becomes eternal. But before we do that, keep in mind that you have to try your best and understand and acknowledge your partner's feelings and emotions. You have to fit in their shoes when the times come and look at things from their perspective, too. You must be open to healthy discussion and conflict resolution when required.

Chapter 2:

Don't Give Them the Silent

Treatment –TALK!

Imagine this: Before leaving for work, you specifically told your husband to put the dirty clothes in the laundry basket instead of leaving them on the bed after he changes into work clothes. You said it a bit sternly this time, because apparently, he'd forgotten to do it the last three times you asked him politely. Hoping that this time would be different and he would at least try to not disappoint, you leave for work.

When you return, not only has he forgotten yet again, the bedroom also reeks—not only had he left these clothes, he left the towel on the bed too along with them. Frustrated and with your blood boiling, you wait for him to get home. But you're not in the mood for a fight or argument. You've already done that the last two times and clearly, it hasn't made much of a difference in the routine. So, you decide to not say a word about it. You give him the silent treatment, praying that it would do the trick.

Spoiler alert: it won't.

There are disagreements between all couples. Sometimes, they're even a sign of a healthy and stable relationship—however, when you start to use the silent treatment as a means of punishment, it can make it a living hell. According to a study in the Personal Relationships Journal, one of the most common patterns that researchers see in couples going through a rough patch is becoming withdrawn from your partner (Papp, Cummings, & Kouros, 2009). This kind of negative behavior is also associated with increased toxicity in relationships, which, again, isn't good for anyone.

During the experiment, the researchers interviewed some 100 married couples in the United States and tried to understand why some relationships turn sour over the years and some don't. The couples that were interviewed had to keep a daily report of their marital status and marital conflicts. They were also expected to rate their depressive symptoms. Several different factors affected the results—such as the age of the couple, how long they had been married, were they friends for a long while before marriage, their personality types, etc.—but when the reports were analyzed, researchers found that a demand-withdraw pattern, common in many report findings, was a big predictor of spousal depressive symptoms and marital dissatisfaction.

This pattern, simply explained, is when one of the partners demands a change in behavior or action of the other partner and withdraws from the confrontation by becoming silent, walking away, or by ignoring that person completely. This demand for change and withdrawal as a response are both behaviors that pave the way for toxicity in the relationship. This pattern does two things:

1. Forces the partner to embrace change
2. Blocks communication with them until the demand has been fulfilled

Thus, silent treatment is never a promising solution to any given situation, as it makes one do something forcefully and not out of willingness, meaning it will eventually be repeated sometime in the future. If we carry on with the same example of leaving dirty clothes on the bed, the husband might put the clothes in the laundry basket for a week, in the hope to not upset their partner, but will go back to doing the same unconsciously or when in a hurry—the point being that it doesn't enforce change, but rather just delays what comes naturally to someone.

The silent treatment is an expression where one partner holds back on the communication—deliberately ignores the person, stops replying to their texts, cancels their calls, and avoids making eye contact until the other partner realizes they have messed up somewhere. Most of the time, when partners use the silent treatment, it is done in the hope of getting back at their spouse instead of expressing how they feel and ending the matter once and for all. This only escalates the matter further and increases the tension between them. Not all partners handle the silent treatment well and may retaliate by lashing out. Therefore, many experts advise never to let this happen in relationships, and instead be open and willing to communicate instead of shushing up.

The nature of silent treatments is manipulative and is designed to receive a response. But what if that response isn't the one we desired? What to do then? Besides, it isn't a suitable solution to resolve issues and should be avoided at all costs. If you have the habit of treating your partner in this manner, maybe it is time to give it up to retain the peace and calm in the relationship.

Why Do We Do It?

Tina Gilbertson, the author of *Constructive Wallowing: How to Beat Bad Feelings by Letting Yourself Have Them* and a counselor in Portland, believes that silent treatment is an amalgamation of unwillingness to talk about something and hurt feelings. Meaning, we feel hurt but we won't talk about it. She related one study by Paul Schrodt in which he reports silent treatment is one of the most damaging things to any relationship (Schrodt, Witt, & Shimkowski, 2014).

According to him, the more polarized the spouses become, the harder it is for them to not engage in the behavior again. This means that if one of the partners begins to look at the silent treatment as a means of achieving desired results, they might begin to use it more frequently, without realizing the consequences it brings with it. After reviewing 74 studies surrounding the same hypothesis, Schrodt presented his analysis in his research study. The analysis examined the data of more than 14,000 participants, some of them coupled, divorced, and widowed. He also revealed that during most of the studies, women seemed to be using the demeaning habit more often (although not always) and men were typically the ones who withdrew from the demands placed. But he noted he doesn't believe in blaming just one party, as both partners have their share of guilt and mistakes.

Therefore, he suggests that both should work together to reach a mutual and constructive conclusion to move out of the conflict and resolve it with maturity. Why? Because it doesn't take long before it becomes a vicious cycle, and before you know it, you're not even addressing the issue at hand but rather just arguing about arguing.

The silent treatment is one of the worst things you can do for your relationship, even if you're feeling angry.

But the question is still the same. What makes one resort to such behavior—especially when the relationship is fairly new? Well, there are some compelling reasons that we ought to look at to understand where this behavior comes from. Before we get into it, note that these aren't the same for all new marriages—these are highly impacted by the dynamics of the relationship the partners have.

They Want to Hurt/Punish You

This is one of the most common reasons for such behavior. Picture this: You were returning home in the wee hours of the morning and arrived to find your partner in a cross mood. You're too tired to argue, and by the time you come out of the bathroom, they've already switched off the light and gotten into bed. Since you are fatigued, you sleep in, too. The next morning, you wake up and don't find them in bed. You pick up your phone to check for notifications, and there it is— it's their birthday today, and they were expecting a call from you at midnight.

The reason for the silent treatment is to let you know that you have hurt their feelings by forgetting about such an important date, especially if it is also the first time you two are celebrating it as a couple. They are also sort of punishing you by not talking to you to show you that you have made a grave mistake and need to apologize. They want you to feel guilty and are hoping to achieve this by playing the victim card.

They Want to Control and Manipulate

It is natural for all of us to want to be loved, looked after, and cared for. Of the many ways we can make ourselves feel as though we belong is when we have people who communicate with us. When someone comes up to us and starts talking, even if just to ask for directions to someplace they need to be, we feel valued, smart, and intelligent. However, if they choose to ask someone standing beside us without acknowledging our presence, it makes us feel less valued and unwanted.

When someone chooses to respond to us with the silent treatment, it is a subtle way of telling us that unless we choose to act, behave, or talk in a certain way, we will not be given the opportunity for companionship and familiarity. That is manipulation and control, right there. So, we can assume that another reason we give our partners the silent treatment is because we wish to manipulate and control some of their actions and behaviors.

They are Seeking Attention

Another reason for giving your spouse the silent treatment is to seek attention. When one of the partners feels invalidated, they may use the silent treatment to let their spouse know how they feel. They ignore when they feel ignored. They stop respecting you when they feel disrespected.

They Want to Inflict Pain

The silent treatment can also be a way to inflict pain— the kind of pain that takes longer to heal. It isn't like a cut or a bruise that improves with time and eventually leaves no mark. It is emotional and can mess up a relationship if we let it.

When your partner chooses to not communicate with you, it is a sign that they are bothered. It's like telling you that you did something wrong but, hey, we're going to let you figure it out on your own. When this continues for long enough, you start to wonder if there is something wrong with you for having hurt them this bad. As a result, you take a step back and pretend to be someone else. You step back from being you and that, clearly, isn't all right.

They Want to Be Taken Seriously

When someone resorts to becoming silent, there is a reason for such behavior. It isn't always a means to get attention or manipulate you. It can be more, especially if the person giving the silent treatment is doing so because they feel that their opinions and values are going unheard. They feel their say doesn't get as much consideration as it should.

This happens often with new couples. One of them feels like the other keeps taking charge of everything, having the last word and not hearing or acknowledging the sacrifices the other partner has made for them. Sometimes, we are so unconcerned with our partner's concerns that we may even mock them over it without realizing how offensive it can be. Take this as an example.

Your partner looks tense over some work-related things. You come up to them and ask them to communicate, hoping that you might help them in some way to resolve the issue. But they jokingly brush you off, saying you're too naïve to understand these things.

Can you imagine how hurtful that must be? It's like saying, "Hey, I don't think you are smart enough to comprehend the complexity of it. Maybe you should stick with the chores." After all, they were just trying to unburden you and make you feel a little relaxed. But that kind of a response from you isn't justified.

They Don't Want to Fight

Some partners hope to avoid getting into fights, so they keep to themselves whenever they feel hurt or neglected. However, frustration can only build up to a certain point—it has come out eventually. When that point comes, some partners choose the silent treatment instead of having an actual discussion or argument with their partners. They don't want to ruin the peace of the house or fear causing damage to their relationship. But, alas, that is where they commit the biggest fault of all. Why? Because silence is more deadly than words. It's a harsher punishment than an argument.

They Are Done!

On the other hand, some partners fight so frequently that, to them, the silent treatment feels like a comfort. Let's be honest, fights are exhausting, especially when you are up against someone you dearly love. But when one or both the partners are fed up with the consistency and want some quiet time in the house for once, they may opt for silence.

Why Silent Treatment Doesn't Work

As powerful and impact-having as this behavior seems, there are several reasons why it fails to achieve the desired purpose. And to provide you with proof, let's take a look at these five points below.

It Can Be Misinterpreted

Picture this: Your spouse has the habit of nagging. He does it about everything. If you clean the house, it's not clean enough for him; if you do the laundry, it doesn't feel soft or smell nice; if you iron their clothes, you could have done a better job.

Sometimes, when we are angry, the only thing we need is some quiet. So, there is a possibility that if the nagger chooses to give you the silent treatment, you might enjoy it.

It Might Go Unnoticed

If you are naturally shy or aren't very expressive about your concerns, your silent treatment might go unnoticed by your partner unless you really put it out there. If they're occupied with other things, they may not even notice that you're not talking to them. Therefore, you will fail miserably and your concerns will remain unheard.

It Can Be Tough to Keep Up With

How long do you expect to stay quiet? It can't last forever, as it is our natural tendency to communicate. Besides, you two share a room, a house, and chores... Eventually, you will have to talk to each other. It's nearly impossible to go on with this for more than a week. What then? If your partner still doesn't apologize or just chooses to ignore it, what are you going to do about it? Will you just give it up? That will make you feel more of a loser than you did before.

It Doesn't Address the Issue

The silent treatment isn't an effective way to handle issues. If you want the problem to get resolved and not happen again, you have to speak about it openly and clearly. Will you keep getting upset and going on silent mode forever? Probably not. Instead, act wisely and communicate, because unless you deal with the core issues, you will only be setting yourself up for a bigger upset the next time.

Even if it works, what happens next?

Now that you have chosen to stay quiet and not engage in any form of communication with your partner, where does that leave you and them? What does it say about your relationship? Will you stay this way forever? Since this doesn't seem to resolve the issue at hand, where do you go from here?

You have to plan and hope for a more promising future for the two of you. So, don't do anything that will tarnish the beautiful life that you have created for yourselves and leave a mark so ugly that you spend your whole lives trying to clean it.

Silent Treatment and Its Impact on Your Marriage

If you choose to employ this technique, it's important to consider the drastic changes it will have on you, your partner, and the holy matrimony that you two jumped into while promising you will get through thick and thin—not to mention how it will be harder to grow back together and not feel hurt, victimized, and accused. Consider this a fair warning from my end to not let your relationship go to ruin because this one-time thing could eventually turn into a full-grown monster, ready to devour the fun and romance from your lives.

For starters, this behavior leads to mental stress. It isn't only the one giving the silent treatment who's going through tough times, the accused also suffers through a whole lot. They have more explaining, apologizing, and sometimes begging to do, which is unfair. They may feel isolated, disrespected, less valued, and excluded. All of these can lead to increased psychological and emotional stress. Besides, maybe you're taking things too seriously here. Maybe you're overreacting. Maybe the reason for your angst is something entirely different, and you're just using your partner as a vessel to release it from your system? But where does that leave your partner? Hell, they might have to submit to you to make things normal again. They may feel pressured into feeling hurt or guilty.

Secondly, it leads to self-doubt. The partner who is going through it all may not understand what's going on. They may have to fight battles in their head to figure out the root cause of the problem. They will have to guess at where they went wrong. Doesn't that seem like a lot of work in the first place? It is also a waste of time, and the longer you remain distant from one another, the more damaging it can be for your marriage.

Thirdly, when acted out repeatedly, this can turn into a harmful habit to demand things from your partner. This is a clear violation of the vows you two shared where you promised each other your complete trust, devotion, love, and respect. The lack of communication damages relationships. Are you willing to give up on it so soon? Think about that for a minute. There are other ways of resolving the issues—ways that actually work and address the problem.

And finally, it doesn't do your health any good, either. Excessive stress can be bad. It can make one feel anxious and impatient, kill one's appetite, and leave one feeling restless all night long. It also prevents you from focusing and can affect your professional life, too.

Responding to Silent Treatment

If your partner is giving you the silent treatment, there are many ways to handle it. You can't let it go on like this, as you are fairly new to the whole idea of marriage and every marriage has its own set of ups and downs. In this final section of Chapter 2, we will look at how to deal with or respond to the silent treatment. There are many things to consider here before making another grave mistake and escalating the anger and hurt.

For instance, the first, sanest thing to do is to find out the root cause of the problem. Dig into the whys. Why is your partner acting this way? Why are they not talking to you? Don't assume that you have all the answers to yourself. You might have no idea what upset them and reach out to them with the wrong apology. It can be hard to figure out what could be going on in your partner's mind, so dig deeper. Go back to the day or time when their behavior toward you was less confrontational, the last time you two laughed about something or got intimate. All these can help you figure out where you went wrong. Perhaps you two went to a party together and she started to act weird on the way home. Did something happen there? Did you make a joke at her expense? Did you act awkwardly? Did you disrespect someone? Did you eat too much, despite her warning you not to? All of these can be great questions to think about, and if you still fail to come up with a sound explanation for the stonewalling, then follow the next step.

Communicate. This might seem like an ironic choice, since the whole debate is about being silent, but hear me out. Whether it's a criminal that committed a crime, a kid angry with his parents over embarrassing him at school, or partners who don't want to speak to you, communication is the best way to resolve issues. Even if talking doesn't feel comfortable and the only answers you get are sounds like "hmmm" or "uh-huh," continue on your quest. It is the only way to come to a resolution and save your marriage. Communication goes two ways. First, you have to be able to speak, and second, you have to listen. You can't just apologize without knowing what you are apologizing for. You have to listen to their unsaid words. Notice their expressions and behavior. What is it that bothers them?

Or, you can use the sandwich method. The sandwich method is a direct approach to give constructive criticism using "I" statements. Approach them with a calm and gentle attitude, but also with a clear head. Take a deep breath and request a chance to make things right. Let them be comfortable first. If they are too hot-headed and try to leave the room, let them. Look for another window of opportunity sometime later in the day.

If they seem comfortable and eager to talk, begin the conversation in a tone that makes them speak up, too. For example, using a sentence like, "I've noticed you haven't been talking to me since ___ days or hours. I must have done something gravely wrong to deserve this, right?"

If they speak up, great! If they don't, continue with the probing. At some point, you will succeed in breaking their silence. The second most important thing is to try to avoid making the conversation about you. You have to make it about them, so they feel acknowledged and heard. Let them know how the silence is affecting your peace of mind, but also theirs, and tell them that you want to make things better for the both of you, not just yourself. Include and prioritize their peace of mind, too. When speaking with them, try to look into their eyes like you really mean it, and once they seem motivated to speak up, don't interrupt them.

Next, if they still hold a grudge against you, don't imitate what they are doing. When both partners resort to treating each other with silence rather than focusing on resolving the issues, the relationship can be in critical danger.

If you have the slightest idea of what they are angry or hurt about and believe that it is all due to a misunderstanding, don't waste time before explaining yourself and your situation. The sooner assumptions are dissolved and misunderstandings cleared, the better. Maybe the reason you had to cut their call was that your battery was nearly dead. Maybe the reason they didn't cook dinner was that they had a terrible headache the whole day. Maybe the reason they keep demanding attention is that they feel unvalued. If I have learned anything in my whole career working around criminals and victims, it is that every action or behavior has a reason behind it. Your job is to find theirs and see how to address it.

Learn to listen. This can't be stressed enough because often, it is mere neglect that hurts our partners—it's the "not being able to communicate" part that gets them. They want to feel valued, and one way of knowing that they are important is when they feel heard. When the things they say mean something to you. When they don't feel like they're just banging their head against the wall because you keep repeating the same things. Communication is a two-way street. It doesn't just involve talking relentlessly and when the time for your partner to contribute comes, they just shove you away.

So, let them know that you're willing to listen to whatever it is that they need to say.

In case things have gotten back to normal but the issue remains unresolved, take some time, perhaps a while later, to discuss it and reach a consensus on how to deal with it. When you don't do that, there is a possibility that the same issue will once again sprout sometime later, during a fight or when you do something remotely similar. It's best to not leave things hanging like this and address them accordingly.

Mind your tone. Ensure that the tone or words you are using while communicating aren't remotely sarcastic or caustic. You have to make the most of the chance you have been bestowed with to resolve the issue, not aggravate it further. Be gracious and kind with your words so that they know you mean it.

If you think you have been accused wrongly or that the silent treatment is "going a bit far," try putting yourself in their shoes and see it from their perspective. How would you have reacted if someone, like your spouse, had done that to you? How would you have felt? How would you have reacted?

Seek forgiveness. This doesn't mean that you have to give up your pride. If you have wronged your spouse in some way, you better be ready with an apology. This is the least they deserve after all that they have gone through themselves. Ask them to reopen their heart to you and ask them to be more communicative with you the next time. When someone forgives someone, they are allowing them a chance to make things right. If you don't take that chance seriously and act wisely, then maybe there is little hope for you.

Own your mistakes. If they are willing to forgive you, don't expect them to do the same the next time you wrong them. Own your mistakes like an adult and be considerate in the future. Let them know that you acknowledge what hurt them and will try your best to not put them in a similar position again.

And last but not least, don't give up hope. Keep trying to win them over and promise them that whatever you did or didn't do won't be repeated. After all, you are in this together, right? Don't let something so little be the end of you two.

Next, don't let your grudge or ego get in the way. When you go to them to clear things up, go with an open mind. A mind that is ready to accept the wrong you committed. A mind that is ready to not just acknowledge, but change. Grudges, although natural, can be devastating, too. So, if you are the one treating your spouse with the silent treatment, don't do it because it feels good to see them in shame and guilt. Conversely, if you are on the receiving end of the silent treatment, go with an open heart and mind.

Offer them a constructive way to get out of this. Promise to work together to make things better from now on. Promise to not let the other person feel hurt because of something that the other partner does or doesn't do. Promise to always speak to each other and not shut each other off. Offer a constructive solution that will work for both of you.

And that's not all! You have to make time for the amends, too. You have to live up to your promise and do better. You can't just fall out of love and stop respecting each other this soon in the marriage. How do you expect to work through bigger things together when you can't get this out of your way? Think about all that the next time you try to shut your partner out, or the next time you hurt your spouse emotionally. Think about that and your future together, because you clearly won't have one if this continues.

Chapter 3:

Say "I Love You," Don't Take Your Partner for Granted

Scenario: you're cuddling and watching a movie. She asks you how it makes you feel, and isn't it romantic. You reply with a grunt, too drawn into the movie to listen to her, give her a quick peck on the cheek or tell her that you couldn't ask for more. Hurt, she retreats to the other end of the couch, but you're too busy watching the movie to realize something's wrong.

Oops! You almost fell into a death trap. Often, as the relationship progresses, many partners fall into the habit of thinking their partners know that they are loved, even without being reminded every day. But did you know that taking your partner for granted is one of the most destructive things you can do, potentially leading to the end of the relationship?

Still, it is quite natural to assume, as we, humans, have surrounded ourselves with cement walls and cut off all bridges to avoid being seen as vulnerable. We are busy trying to mask our emotions so that no one makes fun of us for being sensitive. We hide when we have been hurt and resort to tactics like silent treatment without actually doing something to improve our situations. And we do this because we want to protect ourselves from all those things that are intense and fierce—love, passion, and pain. But this tight and rigid protection often comes with a price and, mostly, the sufferers are our loved ones. One prime example is taking others for granted and not telling our spouses that they are loved.

Love, whether for a child, parent, or spouse, is a risky business. We will get to the reasons why we fear saying the oh-so-important three words soon, but before we do that, let's establish if this hesitation is a universal affliction. Spoiler alert: it is!

It's clear that humans fear rejection and pain more than love and passion. We walk around in full armored suits so that no one will come up to us and express how they feel about us, because we are unsure of how we would react. But imagine this: What if, for just one day, we put our guards down and allowed love to seep into our lives like the first rays of sunlight in the dark and gloomy sky? Surely, they make a rather pleasant display of how everything in our universe fills with light and brightness.

The omission of expression, especially when it comes to saying, "I love you," is one of the primary reasons for couple quarrels in the first few years of marriage. Although most couples are quite vocal about their love for one another in the first few months—labeled as the honeymoon period—something changes as they settle into their normal routines. The kisses become less passionate, there is little intimacy in bed, and fewer "I love you's" throughout the day.

What happens here is that we start taking our partners for granted. We begin to assume that they don't need to hear that they are still loved every single day. We assume that they must already know, and those three little words are often replaced by other romantic gestures like doing their part of the chores, taking them for a spontaneous dinner date, signing up for some dance class with them on the weekends, etc. True, all these things do depict a similar emotion, it still isn't enough to replace those words. We need reminders now and then, and more so in the first year of marriage. After all, if you stop feeling the love in the first year, there is little hope that you two will survive the next, right?

So, let's begin this chapter with the hope that by the end of it, not only do we acknowledge the importance of saying "I love you," but we close the book, put it aside for a minute, go to our partners, and say it to them right now.

Wait... Am I Being Taken for Granted?

A lot of partners don't realize that their love and affection is being abused. They feel that since every person has their unique way of expressing love, this must be how their spouse expresses it. They want to tell themselves that they are loved, regardless of all the signs in front of them.

In this first part of the chapter, I am going to take you through all the signs that could indicate that your partner is taking you for granted. The reason for this blunt declaration is because every relationship, especially marriage, thrives on how much each person cares for and supports the other. No one deserves to put all their heart into something and not be appreciated for it. No one needs to feel unwanted and unvalued. Both partners have to pitch in equally. Both need to acknowledge each other and make them a priority in their life. If you have been feeling lately that no matter how much you do for your partner, they don't seem to notice (let alone care), don't lose hope yet. There are many ways to rekindle the lost love and spark in your relationship now that it has passed the honeymoon phase. Just be patient and keep on reading—together, we can figure out the best measures to help you through it.

Your Partner Puts Their Work Before You

Is their job their primary concern? Are they always focused on the laptop after coming home from work, or making calls after office hours? If you feel that their relationship with their job holds more value than you, or they seem more driven and committed to that, then it is a sign that they take you for granted. Of course, there will be days when they are super busy with some big pitch or presentation, but if they seemed to make time for you earlier and no longer do so, then they may be taking you for granted. Don't be okay with being the side hustle—share your concerns with them to let them know how you feel.

Your Partner Doesn't Value Your Opinion

Are they always disregarding your ideas and imposing their own on how things should run in the house? Are they always demanding things be done a certain way even though you do them better? Do they never seek your advice or opinion when it comes to making major decisions affecting both of you? If so, then they might take you for granted.

As you are an equal partner in the marriage, they should address every major and minor concern with you first and then go ahead with the plans. They should validate your opinions about things and stop influencing and manipulating you into thinking that they are the smartest.

Your Partner Doesn't Keep Promises

Picture this: You're all dressed up, waiting to go to that new fancy restaurant in town. You've made the reservations and are just waiting for your partner to get home. After waiting a while, you call them up to only hear that they had completely forgotten about it and have gone out with their friends.

What does that say about your relationship? If they aren't keeping their part of the bargain and not living up to their promises, it suggests that they are becoming distant and take you for granted. They know that you will be upset for a bit but will eventually forgive them, so they keep doing it.

Your Partner Doesn't Do Their Share of Chores

If they keep delaying, postponing, or completely forgetting to do them, this shows they are not the least bit interested and responsible towards you. As a couple, you are in this together, and that means you both have to play your part when it comes to the household chores. However, when they keep requesting you to do their tasks, like take out the trash, empty the cat litter, change the light bulb or get groceries so that they can sit at home all day and watch the game, that's a clear sign that they are taking you for granted. They know you will do them eventually and therefore feel unobligated.

Your Partner Doesn't Have Time for You

Or for anything related to you, even. It is acceptable that they are sometimes busy with their own thing and need some space, but if that has become a habit and they casually prioritize other stuff over you, then it means they don't value you or think that your needs must be addressed. Instead of taking you out somewhere, they go with their friends or make plans without consulting you first—they are surely taking you for granted.

There Is Very Little Communication Between You Two

If the majority of the conversation happens at the dinner table and not before or after, it shows a lack of interest. If you always find yourself initiating conversations that mostly conclude in a few words, it suggests they are bothered. If there is nothing meaningful to talk about so early in the marriage, it can become stale and boring very soon.

Your Partner Never Initiates Plans

Are you the one always planning short getaways and yearly vacations? Are you the one doing most of the shopping and making the itinerary? Do they not seem excited and just comply with whatever you have planned? Not only are they boring, but they are also showing you little value.

It can become exhausting if you are the only one pushing things forward, or at least trying to. So let them, for once, act excited or plan something. If they don't, then it likely means they aren't interested in spending any time with you.

Your Partner Cuts Conversations Short

Are they always putting the phone down in a hurry? Are they always walking out on you while you are in the middle of sharing something? Are they always rushing so that you can finish your conversations faster? If so, then they may not value you enough to listen to your thoughts and ideas and have meaningful conversations with you. They will never try to cut the conversations short if they care for you.

Their Friends Are More Important

Have they just canceled on you because some friends from the office decided to head to a new bar in town? Have they made plans for the coming weekend with their buddies or girlfriends? Are they more excited about that one-day business trip than they ever are when spending time with you?

If yes, then they value their friends more than they value you and they likely take you for granted. They think that now that the two of you are married and no longer dating or engaged, it's okay to head off with their friends without consulting you. It's not like you are going anywhere!

Your Partner Doesn't Groom for You

They haven't shaved in months and are less bothered about the acne on their face, or their facial hair and hygiene. They have stopped paying attention to their fitness, and when you tell them that they need to work out or go jogging with you, they just dismiss the idea, saying that you are being too hard on them.

When a partner stops caring about how they look or dress for their partners, it shows a lack of interest on their part. Not grooming should never be an excuse, and if they seem lazy in that department lately then it's possible that they have lost interest in you.

Your Partner Makes Excuses About Intimacy

Forget about initiating—they never even seem to be in the mood to get between the sheets. They're always coming up with excuses about how hard it was at work or how tired they have gotten after all the household chores. Even when it happens, there is a lack of interest and passion in their eyes and the movements feel robotic. With hardly any feelings or initiation from their part, this suggests they have started to take you and your sexual needs for granted.

You Are Used to the Disappointments

If you are somewhat okay with their behavior and careless attitude toward you and your needs, then it is also a sign of being taken for granted. Your relationship should be anything but a disappointment and if that is the case, then you need to re-evaluate your marriage and notice how much your partner is willing to do for you.

They Keep Forgetting Important Milestones

Do they not remember the first time you two kissed? Do they forget your birthday? Do they not understand the importance of the day when you two first became intimate? If these milestones are significant for you, they should care about them and celebrate with you. If they keep forgetting them and later making lame excuses to say sorry, it is a sign that they take you for granted.

Why It's Difficult to Say I Love You

Why do some partners not feel the need to say this often, you ask? Why do they start to assume that you already know their feelings for you? Why do they think that you know how they feel because of all the things you do to keep the marriage working?

There are multiple reasons why some people have a hard time expressing their love, and thus the other person often feels neglected, hurt, and unloved. If we look at these reasons, we will be better able to understand what goes on in one's mind when it comes to saying those oh-so-important three words.

Since it is a healthy habit to let your partner know frequently how much you truly value them—and so they don't think you take them for granted—we must try to develop it within us. We all love love. We all want to be able to feel love and to return the favor. But if neither partner is willing to let their guard down and say it when they feel it, there is little hope that they will make it past the first few years of marriage with a healthy and stable relationship.

Coming back to reasons why some people find it difficult to confess their love for their spouses, let's discuss a few of these below.

It sounds silly

"I mean, she's my wife. Why do I have to say I love you to her? I married her, doesn't that count?"

This is one of the most common answers therapists and marriage counselors hear from spouses. They think it is stupid and silly to say something like this to their spouses because they assume they already know it. Well, even when someone knows it, it still feels good to hear. Using words to express yourself instills love, breeds passion, and makes partners connect on a deeper level. You don't even have to voice it out like a mantra every day! Just whisper it to them in their ears while they doze off or are leaving the door to head to work. It only takes that much.

You're a show, not tell kind of person

You're ready to make the big moves and gestures, but when it comes to communicating how you truly feel about someone, it all goes to ruin. Some partners are like that. They like to show their feelings by romantically doing things, hoping that their partners will get the hint. Although this is certainly exciting, sometimes, all they need to hear is you saying that you love them. That is enough and often means more than any expensive gifts or nights out. It is that little window of communication that makes the bond stronger. Because let's face it, no matter how much you shower them with material things, these can never be more precious than your words. Items can never replace something said with raw emotions. And what better way to start that heartfelt communication with "I love you?" So don't be that show-off guy and become the telling kind of person, because sometimes, that is all that matters.

You didn't grow up in a household where saying "I love you" was the norm

Saying "I love you" to your spouse is often difficult for partners who have been brought up in homes where those words were never used. They either had strict and disciplinary parents who never showed an ounce of emotion in front of their kids, or they had parents who were always fighting. Or worse, they didn't have one or both parents or a stable house to live in, or even know what it feels like to have a family. Childhood traumas, toxic parents, or unstable sibling relationships, etc. can have a deep impact on the personality of an individual. If your partner comes from such a background, their hesitance to say these words to you so openly is understandable.

But here's the thing! This is also the one thing they need to hear the most in their lives. So if they aren't able to initiate it, do the honors. Show them what a healthy marriage looks like, show them how great and wholesome it can feel to have someone love you dearly and, most importantly, teach them how to say it.

Fear of being hurt

When we give someone power over us, we have to be prepared and accept however they choose to use it. They can choose to love us or hurt us. Since there is a 50/50 chance, not many spouses are willing to take that risk. Nobody wants to be hurt or give someone the power to hurt them. Saying "I love you" to someone, even your spouse, can sometimes feel like too much. It's like telling them, "Hey,... you have my whole heart. Treasure it or crush it under your feet. It is up to you."

You worry about appearing way too needy

Admitting or confessing your love without knowing how it will be reciprocated is a big risk. But with your spouse, you should be able to take it without worrying about how it makes you come off. Some partners assume that when they confess love, it shows them as the weaker person, like they are completely dependent on their partners for their happiness and love. They feel it makes them come off as needy and vulnerable, which, let's face it, isn't a nice feeling. It often feels like you are putting the power and control over your life into their hands and willing to be treated in the way they treat you.

Why It's Important to Say "I Love You"

As you have been together for quite some time now and busy in your routine lives, your relationship may have reached a point where you think it's okay to not say "I love you" to each other daily or do other romantic stuff to let them know you still care. But marriage counselors believe that saying it holds the union together. Those three words are what keeps the marriage stable and healthy. Even when you think they already know how you feel about them, this little piece of information makes it all worthwhile, says Ili Rivera-Walter, a family therapist and licensed marriage counselor. She believes that saying "I love you" to your spouse now and then emphasizes care and commitment.

It also communicates a message of stability and trust. It suggests that your love for your spouse is above all quirks, differences, and flaws. It also suggests that your partner loves you and accepts you as you are, and that in itself is a boost of confidence. It further makes the marriage strong and secure. Overall, this helps partners to thrive in and out of the relationship.

Rivera-Walter also believes that it reinforces exclusivity, which strengthens the connection between partners. Since we only say "I love you" to the ones we truly, deeply love, it makes our partners feel special and prioritized. This is important in any long-lasting relationship.

It demonstrates your effort to keep the relationship flowing as smoothly as possible. Besides, it's hard to read a partner's mind and know if they still feel the same affection towards you. Saying it out loud just ensures that love and care because, as humans, we believe in what we see and hear.

It also brings partners closer to each other and opens new arenas to be intimate together. It can set a pitch for great intimacy between the sheets, too.

Another reason to say it to your partner is that there is a heightened chance that they will say it back to you, too. And let's admit one thing honestly here—we all love to hear it. We all love to be told that. It makes our smiles widen, our eyes glitter with joy, and our hearts jump to our throats. It's a wonder how something that takes less than a second to utter can have such a drastic impact on us.

And lastly, the reason you should say "I love you" more and more often is that some thirty years down the road, when you two are old and gray and one of you is near their time to depart, you will regret not saying it enough. You will regret not having told them that you love them with all your heart and wish to turn back the time to say it just once more. So, don't be that person filled with regret and remorse.

Chapter 4:

The Power of Daily Hugs

and Kisses

Sometimes, even saying "I love you" isn't enough. You have to go beyond that and up your game to keep things going smoothly in the first part of the marriage. Where "I love you" is a feeling, hugs and kisses are the physical testament of it. They are as important as saying the three words—and if you didn't already know, there are some great health and emotional benefits that come along with it, too. In this chapter, we shall learn of not only the importance of physical affection, but also how many hugs married couples should share daily. Yes, there is research-based evidence supporting a certain number, and we shall share that with you later in this chapter.

But first, picture this: It's 6:00 a.m., you haven't slept well, and you have to go to work. Your partner gets up to make you a sandwich and wish you a good day. Worried about the day ahead, you make your grand exit and mumble "have a good day" on your way out the door. Only in the car do you make the realization that you should have kissed them goodbye.

We always think there will be more opportunities, but what if there isn't? What if it was the last time you saw them? Who knows what life has in store for you or them? Would you be able to live with regret?

As such, kiss them as often as you can and hold them close to your heart to remind them of their place in your life. There are tons of meanings behind these two simple gestures.

What Does a Hug or a Kiss Mean?

There are many interpretations of what these actions mean. It can denote hot, burning passion, like in the rainy scene in the movie, *The Notebook,* or it can be milder, like a soft peck on the cheek while she does the dishes and you help with the cleaning of the table. It can be sudden and unexpected, or routine. It can come in the form of a bear hug with both partners clutching their hands together on each other's backs, or a side hug to show spur-of-the-moment affection. It can be intense, where you two just collapse into each other, or it can happen when you both leave for work in the morning. The point being, no matter what form it comes in or at what time, physical affection holds such a special place in our hearts. It's like the world stops spinning for a second or two and the rhythms of your heartbeats match together. If only we cherished each hug so compassionately, alas!

Since both these gestures are non-verbal means of communication, here are some ideas of what sublime messages they hold:

- "You should know that I value nothing more than you. I love you today and forever."
- "Whatever challenges and hardships life throws at us, you will always find me standing by your side for support."
- "I value all that you do for us and our marriage."
- "I don't say this often enough, but I fall in love with you more and more every day."
- "I can't thank you enough for choosing me as your life partner and I will continue to live up to your expectations."
- "You are the best spouse/friend I could have asked for. You understand me like no other and see me when no one else does."
- "It is us against the world—today and always."
- "I love everything about you. I wouldn't dare change a thing. I accept who you are and what you represent."
- "I will love you even when we are worn out, with gray hair and no teeth."
- "You make me feel so strong and confident. You are my rock."
- "I just love how I can come to you and have a clear head. You make my world better."

Reasons to Hug and Kiss More

Why are these small actions important or beneficial, you ask? Well, as promised, here are the many emotional and physical benefits of hugs, kisses, and intimacy in the marriage.

Hugs and Kisses Promote Happiness

Oxytocin is a chemical also referred to as the cuddle hormone by scientists and medical experts. The higher its levels in our bodies, the stronger we feel the urge to snuggle and kiss our partners. It makes us want to stay in constant contact with them and sit close to them when we are together. What many people don't know is that the same chemical is also linked to one's happiness and reduction in stress. Ever wondered why you just felt like all your worries went away with a hug? Well, now you know. It makes us forget our pains and experience happiness, even in the most uncertain of times.

Oxytocin has a strong effect on women, especially, and research proves that women with stable and healthy relationships have more oxytocin in their systems. They also report frequent hugs from their partners and can transfer the same effect on whoever they are with— such as their partner and their children.

It Keeps Your Heart in Great Health

According to one study conducted at the University of North Carolina, hugs reduced the pressure on health and prevented stress (Light, Grewen, & Amico, 2005). For the experiment, 59 women between the ages of 20 and 49 were called in with their partners, boyfriends, or spouses they had been with for at least six months. First, all the women were seated alongside their partners and instructed to spend a few minutes thinking of a time when they felt especially close. Then, they were made to watch a romantic video, followed by some talking between them for a few minutes. The session ended with a 20-second hug. But here's the catch—not all women were told to hug their partners, only some of them. Then, the partners were asked to leave the room and the women were asked to prepare and record a short speech about things that made them angry or upset about their partners in general.

According to the findings, the women who had received the 20-second hug were less critical of their partners. They also reported lower blood pressure during a stressful task. Those women were called in for another interview and asked if they received hugs from their partners frequently or not. Turns out, they did and thus, their oxytocin levels were higher.

They Improve Immunity

If we look at it from a healing and spiritual angle, we notice that when we hug, it puts pressure on our sternum which emits an emotional charge. This activates the Solar Plexus Chakra, which leads to the production of white blood cells in the body—essential to fight off diseases and infections. It also stimulates the thymus gland and helps build stronger immunity, which prompts the healing process.

Hugs Reduce Stress

It is also proven by research that hugs and kisses can be great stress-reducers and lead to a happier and stronger bond between partners.

According to one study, scientists investigated the effects of a hug on the body and how it helps soothe our system (Murphy, Janicki-Deverts, & Cohen, 2018). As it turns out, people who are hugged more often by their partners are less affected by conflict exposure—meaning they can remain calm and composed when faced with conflict later in the day. The age or gender of the huggers didn't matter, and their relationship also didn't have a drastic variation in the results.

Michael Murphy, one of the lead authors of the study, believes that this is because when we hug each other, we deactivate a certain region of the brain that regulates our response to threats.

Therefore, when we are exposed to one, fewer hormones are released by the brain, causing less stress. Less stress also leads to less stress on the heart and other organs that remain calm and function normally. We feel safer, and that in itself is a health and well-being booster. We are less reactive and face potentially-threatening experiences with a calmer mind.

Hugs Promote Better Sleep

Non-verbal physical contact is also linked with a better quality of sleep. There are uncountable benefits of a good night's sleep. You wake up feeling less groggy, have improved mood, experience reduced stress, and see improved focus and concentration, etc.—all thanks to the many hugs you get from your partner.

Hugs Prevent Illnesses

Another study consisting of 400+ adults suggests that hugging reduces the chances of an individual falling sick (Cohen, Janicki-Deverts, Turner, & Doyle, 2014). During the research, scientists studied the medical records of the participants and concluded that the ones with a stronger support system were getting less sick annually. When compared with the record findings of those without a strong support system, they also showed less severe symptoms of illnesses.

Hugs Improve Mood

When you hug your spouse for a mere five to 10 seconds, their body releases serotonin, which is the body's feel-good hormone. It makes our mood better by inducing feelings of happiness, joy, and satisfaction.

Hugs Make One Fearless

Maybe not entirely, but there is sufficient evidence to suggest that it prevents the onset of anxiety and promotes calm (Koole, 2013). It also helps people with low self-esteem and panic attacks. And this isn't just true with humans—children who are used to hugging teddy bears also seem less fearful.

Hugs Help With Pain Reduction

Some forms of touch, such as a hug or kiss (on the lips, cheeks or hands), have the potential to reduce pain (Denison, 2004). During one study, several fibromyalgia patients received therapeutic touch treatments. Each of the treatments involved some form of touching on the skin. Patients, after several sessions, reported a significant reduction in the intensity of their pain and improved quality of life.

Hugs Help Partners Communicate Better

We live in a world that relies more on verbal communication than gestures and expressions. This is one reason why it is much easier to say thank you than to hug someone. But scientists have discovered that humans are more expressive when they touch each other's bodies (Hertenstein, Holmes, McCullough, & Keltner, 2009). The feeling and receiving of emotions are heightened and we can express ourselves better. This also applies to emotions like excitement, sadness, or sympathy. In general, hugging feels quite personal and comforting.

On top of these health benefits, there are also many more reasons to hug and kiss your partner, such as how great kisses are to make up after an argument, or how it allows for some intimate bonding times. It also shows that you care, appreciate, and cherish your spouse. It is an informal and often spontaneous form of communication that makes everything seem less worrisome. It also shows that you value them with gestures other than plain words. Besides, they take less than a minute of your time, so you don't have any excuse to disregard this valuable piece of advice. Take it and make it a habit. Even if your spouse tells you that they hate how you jump onto them from behind and enclose them in a surprising and unintentional hug, don't give up. Because they are probably just jealous of how comfortable you can be when it comes to expressing yourself so openly and passionately. Trust me, they love them, so keep them coming!

How Many Hugs a Day, You Say?

As shocking as it seems, researchers have invested their time and resources to figure out if there is a certain number to denote how many times a couple must hug per day in order to stay committed. This piece of research comes from Virginia Satir, a family therapist who studied and observed numerous couples and suggested hug therapy. According to her research, humans need at least four hugs per day to survive, eight to sustain a healthy relationship, and 12 hugs if they want to grow as a couple.

It seems like too much, right? Well, physical contact in humans and how it affects their lives and relationships has long been a favorite topic for researchers. In fact, during one experiment conducted by a group at UCLA, it was noted that increased physical contact reduced stress-triggering stimuli and chemicals in the body.

For the experiment, the researchers called in several participants, along with their partners, and exposed them to controlled electric shocks. Some of the participants were asked to hold the hands of their partners, while others weren't. The brain images of both the groups were scanned and it was revealed that physical contact helped the participants deal with the pain of the shock and the stress before the experiment even began. When the participants knew that their partners would be alongside them throughout the experiment, holding their hands, their levels of stress also declined. They felt more relaxed and composed and seemed less fearful.

Coming back to the topic, how are you going to squeeze in that many hugs in the day when you two hardly get any time together? Let's see.

- The first hug comes upon waking up. Making out and having sex in the shower also counts.
- The second hug as you two get dressed for work.
- The third when you prepare breakfast.

- The fourth when you two leave for work. A kiss may be appropriate here, too.
- The fifth hug when you two return from work.
- The sixth and seventh in between chores like cleaning the house and prepping for dinner.
- The eighth when you are done with the dinner and just chilling out watching TV. It can be substituted for some cuddling and snuggles, too, as you watch your favorite show on TV.
- The ninth hug comes when you munch on to some late-night snacks or get busy preparing things for the next day.
- The tenth hug comes when you two get ready for bed.
- The eleventh and twelfth—and thirteenth and fourteenth—happen when you get naked and make love.

It seems legit, but what about days when sex isn't on the table as both of you are too tired? Or days when you just order some pizza and eat it straight out of the box because you're too lazy to cook and clean the kitchen? And what about days when one of you decides to go to bed early and the other one stays awake, all alone in front of the TV?

For such days, Virginia Satir suggests that you resort to eight hugs, as that is what is required to maintain a healthy relationship. Eight hugs sounds more manageable and realistic in my opinion, too. But hey, if you want to make your own rules here, go ahead. Challenge the status quo. Just be sure to aim for a higher number, and not the other way around.

Chapter 5:

Learn to Listen, Don't

Ignore What's Being Said

Scenario 1: You're arguing. You tune out, thinking about the movie you watched last night, and forget what they are saying. You simply don't want to engage because you've heard the same thing time and time again.

Yes, this happens in most relationships. Couples tend to tune out when preached over some awful habit of theirs, because they've heard it too many times. A simple example of this would be partners arguing over the fact that one decides to stay out late at night, they don't let the other know of their plans. This can set the stage for arguments to happen, and when they happen too often without the partner doing something about their habit, they just choose to ignore what is being said and zone out.

Scenario 2: Your partner is saying something, and you interrupt to finish their sentence. That's how well you know them, you don't have to hear what they have to say! Or do you? You feel you already know where the conversation is leading, and since your partner is taking too long to get there, you do it for them, assuming the conversation will end sooner. But is it the right thing to do?

"You never listen to what I have to say," or "could you please stop interrupting?" are two of the most common complaints between married couples. When counselors ask partners what they desire most in their interpersonal interactions, many refer to these two as the biggest hurdles to proper and meaningful conversions. They feel that when their partner chooses to ignore or interrupt, they feel unheard, unseen, and invalidated. Couples who don't prefer to communicate about things and have their own separate lives and interests are less happy. Think about it—you don't need any research to prove that. It just seems common sense. When living together, sharing the same house and room, you can't expect to not communicate. When that happens, both the partners may feel unappreciated and unheard. How can that be labeled as a successful marriage?

So, the next habit for a healthy marriage is active listening. Knowing that what you say and mean is heard and understood can be one of the greatest gifts to give to your spouse.

Understanding What Active Listening Is

Active listening is imperative for all relationships. It is a skill that everyone must develop and nurture. It is what makes communications seem two-way and eloquent. When the speaker knows that they are truly being heard and understood by the receiver, it also improves the shared bond between the two of them. But what is it, really, and how is it any different from listening in general?

Active listening, also referred to as reflective listening, is empathetic in nature and suggests giving someone your complete, devoted attention. It is more than just hearing things, but rather validating them and the feelings associated with the statement, too. It is about putting on another's shoes and seeing things from their perspective. It is about feeling what they are feeling, going through what they are going through, and being completely present both physically and emotionally.

The reason this is important in relationships is becoming more evident—in our fast-paced world, where a notification on our phones is enough to distract us, active listening is the only thing that keeps us devoted and engulfed. When we are willing to hear, truly hear, and experience things that the speaker is expressing in a calm, relaxed and composed manner, we do so without judging them or interrupting them. We hold on to our advice and opinions unless requested and let the speaker relieve their burdens.

Do You 'Listen to Understand' or 'Listen to Respond'?

Another problem with listening is that despite communicating, some partners still feel unheard. The things that they converse about or the habits that they are worried about remain unchanged, which leaves the partner wondering if the conversation had any real value.

Most of the time, we are listening to respond and not listening to understand. There is a big difference between the two, which was further studied by Faye Doell. He described two types of listeners: ones who listen to understand and ones who listen to respond. Those who fall in the former category experience greater satisfaction than those who are just waiting to respond. Waiting to respond refers to trying to fix things instead of just listening. Sometimes, we just want to be heard and not hear suggestions or advice regarding the course of our plans. We just want to unburden ourselves and feel a little less overwhelmed by emotion. People who try to fix things, instead, are focused on their own needs. They want to feel like the savior—someone who has all the right advice to offer. During one study, research findings showed that most men try to fix things, whereas women just wanted to be heard and understood.

According to American psychologist Carl Rogers, one of the founding members of the humanistic approach to psychology, active or reflective listening is at the heart of all healthy and stable relationships. It is that one thing that promotes growth and change. People who feel heard are more open, democratic, and less defensive. One of the biggest qualities of an active listener is that they don't make judgments and provide the speaker with a safe and comfortable environment to share their thoughts and feelings.

When we listen actively to someone, we are letting them know that we care about them and whatever they are saying. When we listen to someone actively, we tell them that we are there for them "if" and "when" they need us, and until then we are happy to wait.

The Power of Active Listening

According to Kate McCombs, sought-after relationship and sex educator who travels the world talking about sexuality, empathy, the importance of communication and consent in relationships, creator of Tea and Empathy workshops and the founder of Sex Geekdom (an online global community that gathers all those people who love to have geeky conversations related to sexuality), active listening is highly powerful and crucial to establishing healthy married relationships. During one workshop, she emphasized the following points while addressing the importance and role of active listening.

Don't be a passive listener.

To practice active listening, one partner should check in with the other to ensure that what is being said is also being properly understood. It involves being in the present—and fully present—while supporting the speaker. One primary difference between traditional listening and active listening is that in active listening, we aren't only ingesting new information but also processing it at the same time to comprehend it better. This kind of listening, where the receiver is as engaged as the speaker, takes conversations to a whole new level.

On the other hand, when someone is a passive listener, they simply listen rather than react to the speaker's conversation. The result is more of a one-way communication, unlike active listening. Here, the listener doesn't pay much attention to the non-verbal cues, body movements, and facial expressions of the speaker. Your partner may not feel better if you happen to be a passive listener only. You have to engage and react more to let them know they are being heard, not just listened to.

Active listening eliminates blame.

When one partner comes to the other with a problem, it is quite natural for the other to offer advice or suggestions. However, sometimes, all they need is to vent to an avid listener. They instantly feel better once they have it out of their systems. When we allow our partners this freedom, they can often come up with a solution on their own—which, somewhere down the line, releases you of any future blame, which is sometimes the reason for two partners to drift apart.

Active listening paired with empathy for the partner can create a deeper bond. When you think about it, both listening and empathy require the listener to stay engaged. Each of these practices enables us to listen and understand the feelings and emotions of the speaker. When combined, they become a communicative superpower. This can lead to an improvement in the quality of interpersonal relationships between partners.

Active listening creates a safe space.

When we give our partners our undivided attention, we allow them to feel safe and be more expressive when sharing their feelings and emotions. They know that they won't be judged, and neither will their actions come under scrutiny. This is very important in relationships. Both partners should feel open and communicative and not hide or veil their emotions. They should rely on each other and not others to feel heard and safe. Luckily, active listening offers just that.

Active listening helps you deal with difficult conversations.

Although there is no certainty that the conversations you two will have will be comfortable, it will be easier to discuss them more expressively when you know that your partner is listening to you actively. You won't be judged or made to feel uncomfortable. You won't be looked down upon or feel like your partner is secretly holding grudges against you. You will just be heard and later listen as you two work together to get past any uncomfortable situations as a team.

Active listening cultivates intimacy. As humans, we all want to be seen, understood, and heard. This need often goes unmet in relationships, when one partner feels a deficiency in what they are giving and receiving. They are willing to listen, but they don't feel heard. When we can express ourselves openly and offer critique and suggestions to improve the existing relationship, it can be highly nourishing.

What Happens When You Don't Listen?

The reason we sometimes feel so distant from our partners is that we don't know how to listen actively. You see, not every communication happens via verbal expressions. Sometimes, we have to rely on the non-verbal cues and gestures that our partners give us to understand what is going on in their heads. For instance, if your partner is repeatedly requesting that you turn off the TV or at least lower the volume, it can mean several things. Maybe she has a headache, is preoccupied with something, trying to concentrate, or simply wants some time for peace to herself.

It is up to us to take that hint and do as required and check in on them. Sometimes, people don't express themselves because they don't want to be bombarded with opinions and suggestions on how you can make yourself feel better. Sometimes, they just want to be left alone.

You can only decipher this if you listen and observe without judgment. But not all partners get that, and this is where the relationship starts to crumble. Let's take a look at what happens when partners don't listen to one another, or simply listen but choose to ignore it.

Lack of Clarification

Active listening isn't only about being attentive. A good active listener must be able to unlock the hidden messages. They shouldn't just hear what is being said. They should take note of what hasn't been said but expressed via their partner's tone, pitch, and gestures. A lack of clarity can be a bigger problem in relationships because the subtle hints go unnoticed and thus, the issue isn't resolved.

Increased Conflicts

If one partner keeps on suggesting or requesting something and the other keeps dismissing it, conflicts are bound to arise and feelings will be hurt. Some poor listeners take what is being said to heart and begin to argue or disapprove without even hearing the whole of it. This not only disrupts the communication but also eliminates the chance to resolve the issue. This happens when the listener isn't listening but interpreting the suggested requests as insulting or degrading. This means they respond emotionally and try to blame the speaker, hurting them further—only this time with intention.

You Repeat the Same Mistakes

When you don't listen to your partner attentively, there is also a heightened chance that you will repeat the same mistake over and over again, which is only going to piss them off or hurt them further. If you want some peace in the house, you have to listen to your spouse attentively when they request if you two can talk.

Poor Interpretation

Sometimes, the listener interprets the communication incorrectly. Although they hear what is being said, they make assumptions and mold the words to fit their preconceived notions. This leads to negativity in the relationship, as one or both the partners feel guilty and the issues and worries only become bigger.

Constant Interruption

When one partner is deeply engaged in words and emotions, the last thing you want to do is break that tempo. Interruptions also have a detrimental effect on the marriage as the speaker feels like what they are saying isn't important enough. Some partners make the mistake of engaging themselves in things like looking at their phones, turning on the TV, or getting up in the middle of the discussion and doing something else without realizing its impact on the speaker. If you value them dearly, which I know you do, give them your time and your full attention so that they can feel less stressed.

Misunderstandings Arise

When you don't listen attentively, the chances of misunderstandings increase. Your partner might have said something entirely different and since you weren't attentive, you went on to assume what it must have been about. This sort of careless behavior can lead to more conflicts and arguments in the future, which is the one thing we want you to avoid.

Becoming a Better Listener – The How-To-Formula

To open your heart to someone and nurture theirs is a lovely experience. But it requires active listening. With technological gadgets, work commitments, and obligations pulling us in all directions, it can be extremely difficult to slow down, take a moment and listen. Listening, something that many assume comes naturally, can be quite hard. How often is it that we lose ourselves completely in something?

The more we listen, the more we hear of the things we never noticed. Listening involves more than just one sense, and requires that we submit ourselves wholly when it happens. So, how can you be a great listener for your partner? Here are a few pointers to help build this healthy habit to sustain relationships.

Be Empathetic

When you listen to someone empathetically, you put on their shoes and view the world through their eyes. It doesn't matter what the conversation is about, you have to approach with empathy. This means that you listen with an open mind, acknowledge their feelings, and withhold your judgments. When someone comes up to us with something bothering them, it doesn't always mean that they are seeking a solution or advice. They also don't want to feel judged. When we listen to our spouses with empathy, we make them feel secure.

Listen, But Without Bias

It is natural for us as humans, not just as spouses, to form an opinion about something. Although many couples speak of sharing common interests, one can expect clashes in terms of choices and stances on certain issues. Therefore, instead of letting them block the road to conflict resolution, allow your partner to finish what they have to say before sharing how you feel about it. Bias, when it comes in the way of listening, can lead to more conflicts and arguments. Let your spouse have their moment voicing their concerns, and later present your own case in a calm and empathetic manner. Let them know that you have a different opinion about it and would love to find a middle ground so that neither of you is left feeling unheard.

Stop Interrupting

Again, another natural thing that the human brain just can't stop doing—interrupting. The second we think that the person in front of us is incorrect or has the wrong piece of information, we jump in to present the right one with pride. But here's the thing—no one likes to be cut off in the middle of a thought. When your spouse is sharing something important with you, try not to interrupt to offer suggestions or advice. They will ask for it when they're ready. Until then, hold your horses and let them finish. Don't break the tempo or get them side-tracked by starting a new conversation about something else. Sometimes, when they are going with the flow, a disruption can mess things up.

Maintain Eye Contact

Doesn't it feel awkward when you're talking to someone and they aren't making eye contact with you? To become a good listener, you have to make eye contact with your spouse as they speak. This doesn't mean staring at them like a hawk, but rather maintaining steady eye contact to let them know you are still focused and engaged. Establishing eye contact makes for a strong impression and makes it easier for your partner to be more expressive.

Look for Subtle Hints

Not everything is spoken. Some feelings are hard to express in words, which is why a good listener must look for subtle gestures and expressions. You can note them in the kind of tone they are using, their pitch and quality of voice (if it's breaking or not), hand movements (frequently putting their hand on their forehead can hint at anxiety and worry) and head movements (nodding, or a lack of it). All these, although not explicit or intentional, can leave the listener with a better idea about the emotional state of the speaker and help them create a mental note and respond accordingly. So, stay alert!

When in the middle of an important conversation, a good listener never picks up their phone to check notifications, or dozes off to think about something else. They stay engaged and avoid getting distracted. Even if they see any distractions around them, they choose not to indulge in them. If you want to be a good listener, do the same!

Mirror Them

Mirroring is a great technique to use when listening attentively to your spouse. This doesn't mean you start mimicking their hand gestures, but rather that you reflect the same tone as they use and employ a similar speech pattern. You can also repeat what has been said to you. This lets your partner know that you get it.

Probe Questions

If you have lost sense of their words or believe that you have not understood something they said, don't be afraid to seek clarity. Sometimes, you get so caught up in your emotions that you stop making sense of what you are saying. This can be hard for the listener to track and take note of. Probing questions to better understand where you are coming from can help both partners be aware of what is happening and devise their next plan of action. Begin with repeating what they have said, preferably in your own words, and then add an open-ended question to let them give you more insights. To avoid interrupting, make a mental note of any follow-up questions to ask once they are done with their share of the talk.

Most importantly, let your partner know that you are here to talk and listen to them whenever they need to unload. After all, you are their spouse, perhaps the closest person to them. They should never feel the need to look to others for emotional support.

Communication and listening are healthy habits to keep your marriage going strong. They are especially critical in the first year of marriage, as partners are only learning to accept the many habits and behaviors of their spouses. So, take the time to devote to yourselves. Set a time over the weekend to just talk about the two of you and see how each of you is doing. Discuss things that bother you about your partner and ask them the same. Talking about expectations and paying attention to what is being said is a healthy way to sustain relationships.

Chapter 6:

Don't Bad-Mouth Your

Spouse

Scenario 1: You go out with the girls, have a few drinks, and you start talking about men. Before you know it, you're telling them about the silly things he does or that night when sex wasn't a major success (Performance issues? One of you was tired? Poor communication?). You wake up the next morning regretting the things you said, but you calm yourself down by telling yourself it was only "girl talk."

Scenario 2: You're at the office and one of your colleagues has recently moved in with their partner. They are discussing how awful the place looks with hairpins all over the dressing table and hair in the shower drain. You feel like it's all casual banter and begin to badmouth your own spouse. You tell the guys how she rarely combs her hair or flushes the toilet. You talk about how bad she is at cooking and how you have to make excuses to have something delivered every other night so that you don't have to sit through the meal. Later, you begin to feel awful about the conversation and the details you discussed with them.

You feel like you have violated some kind of trust, but remind yourself that you weren't the only one sharing nasty details, so it should be all chill with the guys.

It doesn't matter whether you express a negative sentiment in front of your spouse or somebody else. Bad-mouthing your partner is never okay, and it can have long-lasting effects on the relationship.

Why Do We Bad-Mouth?

There are several reasons why we choose to bad-mouth our spouses to others. It's more than just a fun thing to do. There are some deep and insightful reasons why we resort to behavior we know can end us in a bad spot with our partner.

The first reason we bad-mouth others, especially in a new marriage, is that we want to please our partners. We want to accept them for who they are without pointing out their flaws, even when they bother us enough to stress us out. So, we turn to others to vent our frustrations, because we fear they will lead to negativity in the relationship. We don't want to be in their bad books or make them feel like they aren't good enough for us. But because we still need to get those thoughts out of our system, we turn to our friends and family members.

Another reason we do it is that we don't want to argue about it. Again, the worry is disrupting the peace and stability in the relationship. We fear that if we begin to address issues openly, it might lead to a fight or disagreement. No one wants to willingly enter a heated debate. So, we just avoid it, and choose instead to share it with people who won't fight with us over it.

Thirdly, as stated earlier, some partners just want to blow off steam. Maybe you're having a bad day and your partner starts to get on your nerves (although they are just being themselves). Since you don't feel like talking to them, you turn to others to get it off your chest.

And finally, some people, especially women, feel that bad-mouthing spouses gives them something to bond over and talk about. Tell us this: Have you ever made a new friend bad-mouthing your spouse or grumbling about the broken coffee maker at work? Complaints give us a reason to chat.

The Dangers of Trash Talking Your Spouse

As humans, we are all born with the tendency to gossip and complain. We make mistakes, and so do our partners. Some mistakes are easy to overlook, but others get inside the head and mess it up. They are too big to be overlooked, and thus we complain about those behaviors. To put it simply, it is impossible to live with someone and like everything about them—it just isn't going to happen.

However, how you choose to deal with this is an ever-sensitive issue we need to address. Despite knowing how effective communication between partners can resolve issues, we still avoid confiding in our spouses about the things that irk us about them. We always choose to avoid having "the talk," and instead share these complaints with others. This is very common when dealing with a spouse who repeatedly makes the same blunders over and over, and you feel like you are done with pointing it out. The frustration that builds up within you leads to dissatisfaction and unhappiness and thus, we look to vent to someone other than them. This is where family and friends come into the picture. They become our shoulder to cry on.

Little do we know that sharing personal details about your married life with an outsider has a ton of dangers—even when they are our parents and siblings.

If you are looking for a straightforward reason as to why you shouldn't do it, let's discuss a few.

It feels like backstabbing. If they found out that you had been bad-mouthing them behind their backs, they would feel immensely hurt, disappointed, and embarrassed. Try to imagine yourself in the same situation. How would you react if you found out that your partner had been making jokes with their friends about you and your way of doing things?

Touché, right?

Therefore, if you don't want to make them feel unvalued, unworthy, and embarrassed, you'd better focus on working out your issues together instead of complaining about them to others.

What other dangers does this bring? Let's take a look!

Secrets Get Out

Not everyone is a great secret-keeper. So, anything you say behind your partner's back may be used against you. Are you willing to take that chance and have your spouse afraid to trust you again? If they find out, they might dredge this up every time you two have a conflict. They may also hold a grudge against you, and your perfect marriage tapestry will be destroyed forever.

People Try to Fix Things

Secondly, some people, upon hearing something bad, will try to fix things for you. They may talk to your spouse to try and amend things between you two. Your spouse will be hurt that you never came to them to discuss it in the first place, and they might feel that they are not good enough. You'll need to make some hefty apologies to get things back to normal. And even if you promise your partner that you will never do it again, they won't take your word for it. They will constantly be worried about you doing it again because you did it once, and that will ruin your marriage, too. They will always feel like they are being lied to and cheated on. Trust is one of the most sacred things between couples. Are you sure you want to risk it and destroy your marriage so soon?

It Isn't Fair to Them

Third, don't forget that when you bad-mouth your spouse, you are talking about someone you live with, spend hours with, sleep with, eat with, and share a bed with. This is the person who makes your house a home. They are the ones who accompany you wherever you go and help you out with the chores. They are the ones who contribute financially and help you pay the bills on time. Instead of appreciating the things that they do for you, are you going to harp on the stuff they don't do with an outsider? It doesn't seem fair. Ever heard of the phrase "don't shit where you eat?"

The Problems Become Bigger

There is also the possibility that this will lead to actual resentment between the partners. In science, there is the belief that if one keeps repeating something over and over again, they start to believe in it. This is called visualization. It's like telling an innocent person that they murdered someone every single day, and there will come a day that they will start to believe it, too. It may take years for some, but it happens. The point is that when one of the partners chooses to talk trash about their partners with someone other than the partner themselves, they are making no effort in trying to change the situation. As they haven't communicated the issues with their partner, the spouse has no way of finding out that there is a problem, and thus keeps on doing whatever is causing the issue in the first place.

The problems eventually become bigger and harder to overlook. They keep testing your patience, and there soon comes a point that your blood starts to boil and this is all you think about. You begin to feel hurt because you think your partner isn't making any effort to change their behavior and become frustrated because of unmet needs. Your mind plays tricks on you and you conclude that maybe you two aren't compatible and that your partner deliberately does things to piss you off. The stories in your mind keep building up and there comes a point when you start to feel resentment toward your spouse. You start to treat them unfairly and get upset with them over every insignificant issue. This leads to both of you feeling unhappy in the marriage.

It Reinforces Negativity in a Relationship

Similar to visualization, it is another idea that whatever we feed our brains with, we begin to radiate and attract the same. Remember the law of attraction? Do you know how it works? When you bad-mouth your spouse over some drinks with your friends or a visit to your parent's house, you reinforce negativity. Marriage is a delicately woven thread. Negative talk is one of the many things that adds pressure and increases the chances the thread will break. The more you talk trash about your partner, the more your brain will reinforce the thoughts. Ultimately, it will become harder for you to see beyond their shortcomings and everything about them will start to bother you.

Creates a Negative Image of Your Significant Other

Are you sure you want these people to have a negative view of your spouse in their heads? After all, they are only hearing one side of the story and a distorted version of it, at that. It's wrong to depict your partner negatively in the eyes of others. They will offer you terrible advice, seeing you as a victim. They will encourage you to make rash decisions that may not end well for you. What if they tell you to leave them?

Meanwhile, your spouse has no idea about what is going on and is completely unaware of the issues you hold against them. Doesn't seem too fair, does it?

It's Disrespectful

Finally, you have to admit, it's disrespectful. Again, had you been in their position and your spouse had done something similar, you would have felt completely unvalued and belittled. So, don't do something that will jeopardize the harmonious relationship you have. Even if you two are facing some minor issues, before involving a third person, try to resolve it on your own.

How to Stop Bad-Mouthing Your Spouse

This is going to be extremely hard, as your marriage is fairly new and everyone wants all the juicy details. They will be asking about how your sex life is, when do you plan to start a family, how is your husband/wife treating you, are they any good with the chores, etc. All these questions may not come off directly, but people will try to get some intimate details out of you no matter how much you try to remain quiet about it. And believe me, it won't be strangers or distant aunts and uncles asking for the nitty-gritty—it will be your parents, siblings and closest friends. Saying you don't want to share or discuss the matter with them seems quite rude, doesn't it? I mean, they're your family. They worry about you. Maybe they aren't inquisitive because they need something to talk about—maybe, they're concerned about the way your partner is treating you.

So, how do you tackle such straight-forwardness and avoid bad-mouthing your spouse? Well, here are a few smart ways to go about this.

Dodge Questions About Intimacy

If you think that a relative or friend is being too inquisitive about your sexual intimacy with your partner and you can sense what the coming questions will be like, dodge them by making up a stupid excuse, like you just remembered that you had to be someplace or that you had to do something important and completely forgot. If you're at a family gathering, tell them that some aunt was calling for you and that you need to go to her. Make it believable and dodge the chance for further probing.

Talk to Your Spouse About It

If someone is giving you a hard time by being rather too straightforward, let your partner know that you aren't feeling comfortable and see if they can come and rescue you from there. You can also let them know in case you did slip out some juice because they wouldn't stop investigating—that way, they won't hold it against you.

Call Them Out

In case the probing continues, and your spouse isn't around to help you out, come clean and let them know that you don't feel comfortable sharing intimate details about your relationship with anyone. It might seem rude at first, but if it is necessary, do it. This is your chance to set an unmistakable boundary and keep the follow-up questions at bay.

Use Humor to Avert the Questions

Humor is a great way to deal with difficult and nosy questions without making the asker feel bad about it. Think of it as the opposite of setting boundaries, as it keeps the situation under control and comfortable. For instance, if you're asked when you plan to start a family a hundred times by different relatives, let them know that you two are still figuring out how to do it or something equally funny as, "Well, let me check my calendar for baby-making days… Oops, it's not on the books this year."

You get the idea, right?

Don't Give Them What They're Looking For

This is trickier, but manageable. Instead of answering the question, you offer them another answer—one that is equally interesting. For instance, imagine this: You are at a holiday gathering at your partner's parents' house when you're asked if the two of you are getting along fine and how your partner is treating you. Instead of spilling the beans, answer strategically with something like, "We're doing great. We both are excelling in our respective careers and, oh, would you like to know about the app my firm is developing? It should be out any day now."

Notice how you subtly change the topic and leave them hanging? This is how you make a transition.

Finally, if there is something you want to complain about, instead of doing it in front of family or friends, do so in front of a professional counselor or therapist. No one else can offer you an unbiased opinion and help you sort through your troubles. They can also prescribe some activities to do together and some communication exercises to discuss the issue with your partner without feeling guilty about it and in a way that won't offend them.

Chapter 7:

Stop Comparing Your

Spouse to Someone Else

Scenario 1: You ask your wife to prepare a favorite meal of yours. She tries, but cooking isn't her forté. Instead of graciously accepting the fruits of her labor, you blurt out, "I wish you were a bit more like Mark's wife—she's a master chef in the kitchen."

Scenario 2: You're at a party at your husband's office. Everyone has come with their wives and one of the guys starts praising his wife over how clean she keeps the house. You turn to yours and, in a mocking manner, tell her to please take some notes. Everyone but her bursts out laughing.

It is very common to make comparisons without even realizing how they will be received. What we see in both the examples above is that the intention wasn't to degrade or disrespect your spouse, but somehow, you ended up doing just that. This is how comparisons work their magic. They belittle the receiver and leave them feeling unwanted or unappreciated.

But here's the problem—we can't avoid them. We can't help making comparisons because we live in a world ruled by social media. We see couples glamorizing a certain type of relationship and instantly look at ours. So what if the Kardashians are going on yet another cruise and you aren't. They lead a different life. You can't compare yours with theirs, because chances are, you will feel bad. Hell, they have all the money in the world to spend on yachts. They have more housekeepers looking after the house than actual people living in it. They have established businesses. They have designer dresses and don't have to stand in front of the closet wondering what to wear to work each day. Fantasizing about leading a similar life and then somehow blaming your spouse in the end for the unhappiness and deficit in your marriage is only going to hurt you. If there are any relationship goals that you need to set, then make your own. Surely someone will pick it up.

Additionally, there are many downfalls to comparing your spouse or relationship with others—and that also includes parents and siblings. Sure, your parents were huge fans of public displays of affection and never felt awkward while expressing their love. But your partner might. Sure, your sister's husband might bribe her with flowers every day but if yours doesn't, don't start to assume that they don't love you enough. What about all the other things they do for you?

Therefore, before falling into the trap of comparisons, and ruin your perfect marriage, take a look at the dangers it comes with and where it can leave you two.

Why It's Not Okay to Compare Your Spouse or Your Relationship to Somebody Else's

With technology making dating more and more accessible, it is no longer impossible to find someone potentially better than your current partner. All you need to do is swipe right, and there you go. However, when it comes to marriage, things get a bit complicated. You have just signed a legal contract and sworn to stay committed to each other. You've said your vows, and there is no going back from where you are. If we add comparison into the question, we are only calling for infinite problems. More importantly, when the comparisons are made through the lens of social media, you just know it is all going to go haywire.

When we compare our spouse to someone else, we are telling them that they are not good enough or that we want more. We are forever making them insecure and they start to feel like whatever they do, it isn't enough to please you.

Other reasons include the following:

Comparisons Kill Your Marriage

There is no nicer way to put it, because that is exactly what it does. When you compare your spouse with someone else, you undermine both them and your relationship. It is never okay to joke about how your man doesn't make you feel good in bed and some hypothetical man might. They start to feel like they are in constant competition to live up to a certain standard, which they think they can never meet. Would you be okay if your spouse posted pictures of some hot man or woman on their social media and lusted after them? Would you be okay with it? Would you not begin to compare yourself to them? Wouldn't you feel undervalued, resentful, and insecure about your appearance? More importantly, wouldn't that ruin your marriage?

It's Toxic

It can get nasty and toxic when you compare your spouse to someone else. You get blinded by the perfection of someone else's partner and, in return, turn a blind eye to the good things about your own. You begin to ruminate over the things your marriage lacks and that can lead to resentment and hurt.

You start detesting your spouse for something they have no control over, especially when you are drooling over someone's appearance only. Sure, they can hit the gym and do a few planks, but is that all that is needed to sustain a healthy relationship? What if they build the desired body you want and then leave you for someone else because you chose not to love them for who they were?

When you compare, you add toxicity to your otherwise harmonious life. You start to fixate over something you don't have and it starts to mess with your mind and emotional state. My advice? Don't get into this toxicity and cherish the uniqueness of your spouse and relationship.

It Leads to Insecurity

Comparisons can also lead to insecurity. Think about it—if you are a man and your wife gets thirsty over someone else, wouldn't you feel insecure about yourself? Moreover, you will always live in the constant fear that this is what they value and want, so they might leave you when someone better comes along. Any relationship where either partner lives in constant fear of being left alone can never be a happy one. Both men and women are rather insecure about their physique, so be aware of how these comparisons can hurt.

Your Partner Feels Humiliated

If you look up the word humiliation in the dictionary, you will find that it translates to a painful loss of self-respect and pride. To be shamed by your spouse, especially publicly or on social media, counts as humiliation. It tells the whole world that you wish that your spouse was better. It also tells the world that they aren't good enough and how unhappy your life is with them.

The Reality is Often Distorted

How do you know that the couple you just compared your relationship with is having the time of their lives? So you just saw a picture of them hugging a panda in China on their latest trip. And did they not return from the Maldives a few months back? Surely, they seem in love. And you... stuck with a partner who is more focused on their work than spending time with you.

When we compare our relationship with someone else's, we do so after watching them look happy either at a party or in a picture in our newsfeed. The rest is all the work of our imagination. Maybe they had a big fight right before the picture with the panda? Maybe their trip to the Maldives was suggested by their marriage counselor, who thought it would be nice for them to spend time together and rethink getting a divorce.

The point is, you can never know the whole story about someone's relationship. You only see what they choose to show to the world. So, there's no point in comparing it with yours and messing up its uniqueness. Even your most trusted friends will hide the complex details of their relationships.

You Become Resentful

When you keep comparing your spouse or your relationship to someone else, you begin to resent your partner and your relationship. Suddenly, it's not good enough for you, and you want more. Even the slightest incompetence on their part begins to trigger hatred for them and you feel like you are suffocating.

You Begin to Take Things for Granted

That said, you begin to overlook the uniqueness of your relationship and worry about the things you don't have. You spend hours making a mental list of things your spouse isn't rather than looking at the things they are. The things you should be grateful for. The things that make them unique. The things you fell in love with or married them for. They seemed to be enough for you when they proposed, and you said yes. They seemed enough when you two went shopping for the wedding. They seemed enough when you overcame the wedding jitters because their love and affection was all that you wanted for the rest of your life.

So, what happened? Why, all of a sudden, have you started taking things for granted? All because you saw a drama in which the main character did things that only men and women do in dramas? Stop thinking about how the grass is greener on the other side and worry about keeping yours alive.

You Begin to Have Unrealistic Expectations

If you thought that there was such a thing as the perfect relationship or partner, you couldn't have been more wrong. These only exist in TV shows and movies, and even there, they put up a disclaimer suggesting that all the characters are fictional and don't resemble anyone living or dead.

Since social media hides the ugliness of relationships, you can't measure your relationship there. In fact, there is no scale to measure relationships, because everyone has a different one. However, when you give in to those expectations of perfection, you begin to concoct unrealistic ones in your mind. And then you get caught up in that fantasy and real life no longer seems as pleasing.

You Become Dissatisfied and Jealous

Continuing from the point above, you start to get jealous of the people you or your spouse gets compared with. For instance, if your husband compared you to his mom or one of your best friends, you find yourself feeling jealous of them. Every time you are intimate with them, you can't keep your mind from thinking things like, maybe they are thinking of your friend. If something that they might have said jokingly affects you this much, imagine if they started actually comparing you with others.

Your Partner Gets Discouraged

Dislodgment happens when you lose confidence in your abilities. You lose your passion or enthusiasm. Discouragement, in relationships, refers to the loss of passion. It can also refer to losing confidence in yourself. For instance, if your wife constantly brags about someone else's boyfriend or husband, you start to lose all confidence in yourself. You think that they are not happy with you and begin to distance yourself.

This form of discouragement is natural. When one doesn't feel valued or appreciated and is constantly compared with someone else in a negative way, they start to think that what they do doesn't matter. This is one of the most common reasons why some partners cheat. They don't feel respected or valued by their partners and thus, they look for it elsewhere. Don't get me wrong, I'm not justifying cheating, but you have to own up to your own mistakes when your partner withdraws from you and seeks respect elsewhere.

How to Stop Comparing – Tips That Actually Work!

Now that we know of the dangers, how can you stop yourself from the comparisons? How can you hold onto what you have and not worry about the imperfections? How can you stop complaining about what you don't have and gloat about what you do? Well, in this section, we look at some self-reflecting strategies that are perfect for spouses who resort to making comparisons.

Remember that you married them

First things first, there must have been something special about them that compelled you to propose or say yes when they popped the question. No matter how they have changed over the course of a few months, there must have been a reason why you married them in the first place. Remind yourself of that reason. What made you fall in love with them? What made you choose them over the many others you could have had your chance with? What made you decide to settle down with them?

Focus on that and see if you still hold grudges. Own up to the choice you made so that you can start to accept them for who they are. Surely, you aren't perfect either, and if they aren't complaining, neither should you.

Self-reflect

Are you perfect? Do you think you are everything a man or woman would desire? Are you hotness, personified? Instead of finding flaws in your partner, start with yourself, first. Maybe the reason they behave a certain way is because of the way you are. Picture this: Your spouse keeps making excuses to avoid getting intimate with you. They keep denying your requests for sex and you start to think that they are the problem. They don't want it. They have fallen out of love. They no longer have a craving for it.

All this negativity about your spouse can make you hate them. But what if the problem was with you? What if you only cared about your needs and said no to theirs? What if they always felt used and not made love to, because they never reach a climax and you can't seem to care why? They might have started to think that you only care about yours—or worse, that there was something wrong with them.

Therefore, instead of pointing fingers and comparing your spouse with someone else, I suggest you do a self-check first.

Understand that even the most perfect of couples could be struggling behind closed doors

You never know what is going on in the lives of seemingly perfect couples. You are not with them 24 hours of the day. You haven't seen them having an argument. For all you know, they could be treating each other terribly. You know how people smile for the camera when the photographer tells them that he is taking a picture? Once the picture is taken, they go back to being themselves. Well, relationships can be like that, too. So, don't compare yours with one that you don't know that well.

If you've hurt your spouse, apologize for the mistakes you've made

And finally, if your actions—or overreaction—has hurt your spouse, apologize to them this instant. It is highly unacceptable to make them feel like they aren't good enough in the first place, let alone compare them to someone or something they are not. Maybe it's you that needs changing. If you wanted a hip and happening relationship with your equally hip and happening spouse, you shouldn't have married someone whose idea for a perfect date is going to the library and getting your noses buried in your favorite books.

However, if you are trying to use comparisons to improve them or make them a better human being, then use them wisely—particularly in a way that doesn't seem too pushy or disrespectful.

Accept the reality

Life is no less than a rollercoaster ride. Sometimes you're up, sometimes down, and sometimes on the edge, ready to tip off. It was never meant to be a fairy tale, which means you have to work for it. If you see some shortcomings, you have to compromise. The more effort you make to improve your marriage, the happier you will be. You can't just sit around all day, waiting for things to magically get better. If you think your partner isn't good enough, communicate and let them know how you feel. Give them the chance to improve and provide them with opportunities that make transitioning into a better version of themselves easier for them.

And if they fail to achieve that standard, don't hold it against them. Accept the reality and make the most of what you have. Maybe their circumstances are different than yours. Maybe they have different priorities in life. If I started to list the differences between two couples, it would require that I write another book.

The point being, no two relationships are the same. Maybe the reason someone's husband does most of the cooking and cleaning in the house is because they work from home and their job doesn't require that they come to the office every day. Take a real estate agent, for example. They don't need to head to the office unless they have people they need to show houses to. Maybe someone's wife takes care of the house and the kids so efficiently because she is a full-time parent or has done volunteer work all her life. You see, they may be at a different stage in their lives—something that isn't realistic for you in the time being. So instead of wanting it, accept and make the most of what you have with your partner right now. Just because your partner can't afford to buy flowers for you every day because the finances are tight doesn't mean he doesn't love you.

Embrace the uniqueness of your relationship

As repeatedly stated throughout this chapter, I can't emphasize this enough—you have to embrace what you have. Our uniqueness is what makes us stand out. Just as two people can't be the same, relationships are equally individual. Every relationship, no matter how young or old, has its own dynamics. Therefore, trying to compare it with someone else's is only going to hurt you in the end.

Ask yourself this: have you not been happy until now? If you were, then there's no point in trying to become or want someone else's depiction of a love story. It will ruin yours. If you were happy before this whole fiasco in your head, then don't be bothered. Nothing else should matter. Don't punish your spouse for it, and don't curse your relationship. Someone, right now, might be looking up to you two and wishing they had the same kind of intimate compatibility as you and your partner.

Therefore, instead of picking out the faults in your partner or complaining about the staleness of your relationship, learn to embrace it and enjoy every minute of it. Some years from now, when the kids come along and your family grows, you will reminisce about the time you two had with each other and wish to go back. Don't let comparisons come between you, and accept your partner with an open heart and mind. Let them be who they are without forcing them to live up to a certain standard. Don't nag them over the things they don't do, and appreciate them for the ones they do. When they feel respected, appreciated, and valued, they will want to improve themselves and do more for you.

Chapter 8:

Continue Dating Each Other

What does Saturday night look like for you? Are you in front of the TV watching a football game while she's on her laptop watching *America's Next Top Model*? If you can't remember the last time you took her out on a date, it's time to make a change.

A date, really, Marvin? *That's* what you're suggesting? Well, firstly, this is my book so I can do whatever I want, and secondly, it's more important now than ever to date your partner.

Just because you got married to someone doesn't mean you stop taking them out to fancy dinners, dress to the nines for them, and get drunk talking about your favorite hobbies in the bar. Isn't that what a normal date sounds like?

Dating or courtship isn't just for lovers. It's for spouses, too. It's a fun way to engage with each other. It's romantic and exciting, and it's about giving each other the same kind of attention you gave them when you first met. It's about being a little nervous about what you guys will talk about, and also a bit excited because there are endless things you two can share and discuss over a three-course meal.

We all have this preconceived notion that dating is only about taking your partner out to dinner, but it's so much more than that. It's about spending time with each other, talking about the things you never get to talk about at home, reminiscing about the beautiful past and making plans for an equally amazing future together.

Therefore, in this chapter, we shall discuss yet another healthy habit to add to your happily-ever-after so that you never have to worry about why your spouse has lost interest in you or why the marriage feels rotten and stale so soon.

Continuing to have regular dates is one of the most important things you should do to maintain the excitement and fun in your relationship.

Why Dates Nights Are Important Post-Marriage

Date nights are important for several different reasons. For instance, there is only so much time that you two get to spend with each other on a regular basis. Some days, you rarely even talk about something out of the norm, and that can be deadly. Date nights give both partners some time together where they can open up and share their concerns, worries, happy moments, and plans in total peace. No household chores are waiting to be done, no interruptions pop up in the form of phone calls or texts, and no time wasters to distract you. When you two finally get down to have a moment to yourselves, you begin to learn new things about your partner, too. Additionally, when you plan a date night with your partner, you are telling them that they are important above all. It is going that extra mile to keep the relationship stable and prevent it from rotting.

Secondly, when you go on date nights with your spouse, you also show them that you want to invest in them. Yes, dates can be costly (they don't have to be, but if you want to take things up a notch, go for it) and stressful. You don't just pick the first dish on the menu, do you? No, you take your time to research what offers the best value, looks tempting, and is good for your health. Think about it—if you're allergic to peanuts, would you order something with peanuts in it? The point is, a lot of planning goes into deciding where to date and when. However, if you are willing to go through the hassle and plan a memorable experience for them, it shows that you really care about them. And dating your spouse has other perks, too:

Dates Bring Back that Initial Excitement

Remember the time when you both took hours to get ready for a date? Remember how you curled your hair or borrowed your friend's perfume because you wanted them to find you attractive? Remember how you looked into the mirror countless times, retouching your hair or deciding on whether or not to leave open that top button? Remember the butterflies in your stomach when one of you waited for the other to arrive? Wasn't that exciting? Well, you can experience the same excitement once again.

Regular Dating Nurtures Friendship

Humans tend to change. They can adapt to new habits every passing day and give up old ones. This is one reason why science is always trying to figure out what goes in our heads. Another reason to date your spouse is that they might have changed, too. They may not be the same person you married a couple of months ago. They may have picked up some new habits, tried some new things, and changed a bit.

This means there is always something new to learn about them and nurture your friendship. It allows you to know each other on a deeper level and share your victories, concerns, and troubles. Marital friendship is as important as intimacy. Couples who don't invest time in getting to know each other may also have a hard time getting intimate and close.

It Gives You a Chance to Enjoy Something New

See, it doesn't have to be fancy all the time. If the goal is to simply spend some time together and away from home and work, then visiting a new place just around the corner also counts, as long as you two are equally excited about trying it. It can be a fun or bitter experience—but something that you two will remember.

It Strengthens the Bond

Who, today, has the time to sit and have a deep conversation with their partners? With work getting more stressful day by day and social commitments wearing us down, going on a date may start to seem like the only time you two get away from all the hustle and bustle. A majority of couples that seek therapy and counseling complain of not spending enough time together.

It is no doubt that relationships require work. Like a plant, they need to be watered and looked after. Both partners need to be present for one another to fulfill each other's emotional and physical needs. Going on dates can help with that. When you two dress up nicely, the feelings are bound to come. Being intimate with your partner is also a form of strengthening the bond and when this is neglected, it takes a toll on the marriage.

Date Nights Improve Communication

It is common knowledge that poor communication between spouses is cited as one of the biggest reasons for separation and divorce. It is the reason why some couples fall out of love too soon. Therefore, you two must keep the channel of communication open.

Healthy communication among spouses can be nurtured when couples give each other the time and attention they need. Wait, isn't that what you do on a date?

How Many Dates Should You Go On?

During one study, Harry Benson of the Marriage Foundation offered some great insights about how often spouses should go on a date. To figure out an exact number, the researcher studied the date-night habits of over ten thousand couples, both new and old. After a thorough review, he suggested the following frequencies:

- Eleven percent of couples go on dates once a week.
- Thirty percent of couples go on dates once a month.
- Twenty-three percent of couples go on a date less than once a month.
- Thirty-six percent of couples hardly ever go on a date.

The togetherness of the couples was monitored for the next 10 years, and as it turns out, the group of couples that went on dates at least once a month showed the highest odds of staying together over the years. They reported fewer fights and better compatibility as the top two things sustaining their relationship. Couples who went on dates every week did better than those who never went on a date, but they also reported additional stress related to planning and deciding where to eat and what to do on a date.

But it is too soon to establish that couples who go out on dates are more likely to stay together in the long run.

Continue to Date – But How?

First things first, understand it doesn't have to be something big—a date night can occur at home where you cook a romantic meal for her after she's had a tough day at the office. Or you can draw her a bubble bath to make her feel more relaxed. On the other hand, ladies, you can help your guy by giving them a relaxing shoulder massage with essential oils or agree to watch one of their favorite movies with them.

In case you are still determined on the idea of going out, here are a few great ideas.

Find Common Interests to Plan Dates

When struggling to decide where to go on a date, look at any shared common interests. Perhaps you two like to shop for antiques, are history buffs, enjoy cooking, or have a passion for health and fitness. You can go on a long drive to look at yard sales, buy from an antique or thrift store, go on a weekly jog together, or take up a weekend cooking class. The choices are innumerable, you just have to look for them. Besides, just because the name says date 'night,' this doesn't have to happen only at night. The goal is to keep things exciting, or else you will start to find ways to skip it altogether.

Take Turns Planning Dates

If you think it's too much of a hassle to come up with something unique every week, take turns planning the date. Make it a rule to keep the identity or nature of the date hidden from the spouse so that they are in for a surprise when it happens. Men, in particular, find the planning part rather stressful. Relieving them of some pressure every other week can give them the time to come up with something new and exciting. Besides, when both partners pitch in, it starts a subtle competition on who plans the best date—so you can expect greater anticipation and thought going into it.

Schedule Date Nights in Advance

Be it a concert we have been meaning to attend or a game we want to see live, when we plan things, we feel more excited. The wait keeps us on our toes. Scheduling date nights beforehand is another way to stay excited as you have something to look forward to. Besides, spontaneous plans often don't work well because you can never know when your partner gets called in to the office last minute while you wait for them at home, all dressed up. Therefore, to avoid being disappointed, it is best to schedule your dates in advance and plan other activities accordingly.

Dress Nicely

If you are going on a date, you have to dress up. That is a given. If you are the kind of couple that doesn't like to dress up and are comfortable in your jammies or shorts, fine, but here's the thing: When you dress up, not only does it show that you have made the extra effort, it also makes you feel happy. When you are aiming to have a good night, you have to make the effort to look good, too. Keep in mind that "good" doesn't automatically translate to dressing fancy, it just means getting out of your regular clothes and wearing something sexy for the evening. You should be radiating sexiness, and you can only emit it when you feel sexy, too.

Avoid Controversial Subjects

While on the date, don't get into arguments or disagreements. Keep the conversation light and pleasant. You can always go home to discuss personal grudges and complaints, but make it a point to not bring them to the table. It will suck all the fun out of the date.

Chapter 9:

Make Time for Healthy

Passion

Imagine this: You feel flirtatious, but she's in her panda onesie and ready to fall asleep. You nudge her gently, she tells you that you can have sex the next day because she's just not in the mood right now. The next day, you're caught up in the office and arrive home exhausted, then you fall asleep while she's brushing her teeth.

Our sex life changes after marriage, and there is no lying about it. This doesn't mean it has to decline or become robotic—a change can also mean a better emotional connection and acknowledgment of each other's preferences and choices. It can also mean an improved understanding, where spouses don't hold grudges against one another for turning down the sex because they feel too tired, stressed out, or distracted. It can also mean increased respect for each other's privacy and a lack of need to get intimate.

This is an ideal chance for couples seeking stronger connection, but the need for healthy passion can't be denied, either. No matter how busy life gets, intimacy should always be a priority to sustain the marriage. But what if there is a lack of passion?

Passion is often the strongest during courtship. The sex is new and exciting, and there is more room for exploration and knowing what the other likes and doesn't like. Gradually, this starts to subdue and the novelty wears off. So, this final chapter—or habit—is dedicated to building healthy passion which, in turn, can lead to amazing sex and improved emotional connection between partners.

Starting with some statistics—did you know that out of 1,126 married couples, 56% of them secretly wish for more meaningful sex in the marriage? This was revealed in the findings of a survey by Cosmopolitan.com (Thomson-Deveaux, 2017) among participants ranging from ages 20 to 29. The top-rated reason for a lack of sex after marriage was busy lives and tough work schedules. Second, the end of the honeymoon phase, and third, lack of interest in the partner.

Twenty-four percent of the respondents revealed that they had sex a minimum of four times a week before they got married and only 9% of them said that they continued with the same momentum after marriage. Sex two to three times per week seemed to be the sweet spot for many, but the biggest finding was that 64% of them responded that a lack of sex post-marriage hadn't affected their married life. They listed more happiness and better intimacy, even when it didn't happen quite as often.

So, what truly matters isn't how many times you get it on between the sheets, but rather how meaningful it is. Therefore, as a couple in your first year of marriage, your goal shouldn't be to keep going at the same pace as before, but rather to work on building healthy intimacy with your partner.

Why Sex and Healthy Passion Are Important

Over time, even the healthiest of relationships becomes habitual. Routine slips in and there is rarely time for proper intimacy. Even when it happens, it happens out of habit and usually, one or both partners come out of it feeling unsatisfied. Intimacy not only becomes monotonous, passionless, and identical (military position), but it also loses its unique charm.

This doesn't mean that the couple has fallen out of love or that they will forever feel incomplete and unhappy, it just means that they need to work to find the lost passion. The loss of passion can be highly damaging. Becoming less and less romantic with time isn't natural, which means you shouldn't be okay with it if it is happening. Now is the time to create room for healthy passion to breed and bring back the romance in the relationship.

Why is it important, you ask? Here's why:

- Bonding: It allows you two to become more connected—both physically and emotionally.

- It takes the relationship to the next level: It is impossible not to feel good after intimacy. It just makes the relationship stronger, piece by piece. It is the glue that holds the marriage together.

- Sex releases feel-good and attachment hormones: When we are intimate, our bodies release dopamine and oxytocin (the love hormone) from the brain that further leads to the release of endorphins that are our natural painkillers. So, in a way, the body not only feels loved, it also builds our stamina and improves immunity.

- Lack of sex can lead to confidence issues: Without intimacy, partners may experience self-confidence issues, worries about fidelity, and concerns about falling out of love with each other.

How to Work on Long-Term Healthy Passion

You may come across a hundred articles suggesting ways to spice up your marriage and rekindle the lost spark, but it takes experience and the study of human psychology to understand why it is needed and learn how to make it happen. Before we get into the many ways to help yourselves stay connected to each other and share a deep passion, we need to understand what the term "passion" truly means.

Passion includes the following things:

- A barely controllable or strong desire to be intimate with your partner (not just sex)
- A state of strong emotion or outburst
- An intense desire or drive
- Something that arouses great enthusiasm

Passion is an important ingredient in sustaining healthy intimacy. Without passion or excitement, sex becomes ritualistic and something you just get done to prove to yourself that you still are a happy couple. But if the feelings are missing, how can it be exciting and intimate? Therefore, before aiming to improve intimacy, work on cultivating passion. Once you find that, sex will always seem exciting and passionate.

The most important way to cultivate passion is to stay emotionally-attuned. Any good relationship is built on closeness and intimacy. That closeness is only possible when both partners feel like they are on the same emotional level. There has to be a strong emotional bond between them. The rest just follows suit.

Coming back to building healthy intimacy in marriage, below are some great tips and advice to start practicing.

Schedule sex: Yes, that may seem weird at first, but your appetite for passionate experiences will return and more frequent intimacy will start occurring naturally. When you plan things, you feel more mentally-prepared when they start to happen. The presence of mind about what is happening, how it is making you feel, and what good it will bring can lead to greater intimacy and an outstanding finale for both partners. Besides, the anticipation of it will make the passion build deeper, too.

Communicate your sexual needs: We all go a little overboard with excitement during the first few weeks of marriage. However, when we come back to our routine lives post-honeymoon, we find that sex and intimacy with our partner are losing their charm. One partner may feel the need to be in bed less than the other. This happens when there is a difference in their libidos.

Females reportedly have lower libidos than men. This means that their need to have sex is less than most men—and they may turn down any advances when they are not in the mood. Keep in mind that they aren't to blame, as it is basic biology. Their body isn't as excited as yours, and that is that. The best way to counter this and find a way around it is to communicate about it. It can feel embarrassing at first, but it will save you from hurting your partner when you turn them down.

Change the scene: You don't always have to get intimate in the bedroom. There are many other places to have sex in such as the kitchen, the couch, or the TV lounge. A change of scene will build excitement and thus lead to passionate sex.

Explore different types of intimacy: Sex isn't the only way to be intimate and passionate with each other. Think of a sensual foot massage or taking a bath in the tub. Moments like these can cultivate passion, too. Embrace it in whichever form it finds you, even if you feel turned on watching them do the dishes.

Try dirty talking and sexting: It seems childish to many but sexting and dirty talk during foreplay and sex is another way to keep the partner turned on and interested. Sexting makes the waiting worthwhile and when it finally happens, it is worth the anticipation. It's simple—just send them a text saying what you would like to do to them when they come home from work. It's cute, bold, and sensual. They won't stay a minute overtime, trust me!

Address your insecurities: Often, the reason one or both partners avoid sex is that they feel insecure about the way they look in the mirror. They want to dress in sexy lingerie, but their curves don't allow them to wear it. They want to tuck in their tummies or hide their saggy man-boobs but can't. So, they avoid getting intimate, and even when they do, the thought of how their partner looks at them is the only thing on their mind. No one with a distracted mind can enjoy the greatness of sex. So, work on your form to look your best or own up to it.

Give without expecting anything in return: ...And you will receive! This is very true. The more you are willing to offer, the more you will get. Be open to talking about fantasies and roleplay to mix things up. Sex, after some time, can become monotonous and that is the last thing we want it to be—boring. Therefore, find ways to offer love to your partner in different ways and you will receive more in return.

Conclusion

Relationships in the first year of marriage are just starting to grow. The spouses are naïve and only beginning to figure out what living as a married couple means. There is a high possibility of clashes, which is why every step taken toward the relationship's improvement must be taken with care. Throughout this book, we've talked about multiple hurdles that new couples face at the start of their married life. In fact, if you go back to read just the headers, you will notice that they all list the most common issues during the first year of marriage. Not enough communication, comparisons, partners feeling unheard, giving each other the silent treatment, ignorance toward each other's needs, etc., are all concerns that must be addressed to help partners navigate their way to a healthy and happy married life.

In this regard, we looked at several habits—along with the effects of the implementation of those habits—to convince the readers to do better. These are habits that will encourage partners to value their spouses more and lead a harmonious and tranquil life together.

This book may not hold all the answers you came looking for, but surely it will be of great help when it comes to surviving the first years of marriage. That, my friends, is a promise. It is for every future wife or husband-to-be, and also for those who have just said their vows to each other and are wondering how to begin their new lives together. *Just Married* shares relatable tips, suggestions, and ideas for overcoming everyday married life struggles to enjoy harmony, happiness, and mutual respect.

Leave a Review

If you loved this book and the information provided, I hope you will carry it forward and help other readers find this book **by leaving a review** for it on Amazon.

References

5 Reasons Why the Silent Treatment Doesn't Work. (n.d.). Retrieved from https://artofeloquence.com/pages/5-reasons-why-the-silent-treatment-doesnt-work

7 BENEFITS OF HUGGING YOUR SPOUSE EVERY DAY. (2017, January 9). Retrieved from https://oneextraordinarymarriage.com/hugging-your-spouse/

Bilow, R. (2013, November 18). Want Your Marriage To Last? Retrieved from Your Tango: https://www.yourtango.com/experts/rochelle-bilow/want-your-marriage-last

Blatchford, E. (2016, July 15). Get Out Your Diary. It's Time To Lock In A Date Night With Your Partner. Retrieved from https://www.huffingtonpost.com.au/2016/03/02/date-nights-important_n_9371110.html?guccounter=1&guce_referrer=aHR0cHM6Ly93d3cuZ29vЗ2xLLmNvbS8&guce_referrer_sig=AQAAAI8fF423TEq_CFP6cJwLZ9bKtmHFwxha-Gw4JQXUfp5IXB5bT4bSgMa5_w7gySpIex

b94vFnfF4cBAg5tx5omt8q1JMQ0crCEmb4
gFL-ibtEaFo-ihbusn7NkDerzkmdm-
vaIuyCtF7W5XxYfHmNiMp1B0IsSdJu2vug
vGH5JSLX

Cohen, S., Janicki-Deverts, D., Turner, R. B., & Doyle, W. J. (2014). Does Hugging Provide Stress-Buffering Social Support? A Study of Susceptibility to Upper Respiratory Infection and Illness. Psychological Science, 135–147.

Degges-White, S. (2016, March 11). Are You Afraid to Say "I Love You?". Retrieved from https://www.psychologytoday.com/us/blog/lifetime-connections/201603/are-you-afraid-say-i-love-you

Denison, B. (2004). Touch the Pain Away: New Research on Therapeutic Touch and Persons With Fibromyalgia Syndrome. Holistic Nursing Practice, 142-150.

Donovan, L. (2019, November 11). 15 ways your relationship changes after the honeymoon stage ends. Retrieved from https://hellogiggles.com/love-sex/amazing-things-happen-honeymoon-stage-ends/

Elle, V. (2018, November 29). 25 Signs That A Couple Has Officially Left The Honeymoon Phase. Retrieved from https://www.thetalko.com/25-signs-that-a-couple-has-officially-left-the-honeymoon-phase/

Feuerman, M. (2020, February 15). 5 Signs Your Marriage Is on the Rocks. Retrieved from Very Well Mind: https://www.verywellmind.com/signs-marriage-is-on-the-rocks-2302504

Fowler, A. (2019, April 12). This Is How Many Date Nights You Need for a Successful Marriage. Retrieved from https://www.theknot.com/content/succes sful-marriage-date-night-study

Fugère, M. A. (2016, May 3). Do Married People Really Have Less Sex? Retrieved from https://www.psychologytoday.com/us/blo g/dating-and-mating/201605/do-married-people-really-have-less-sex

Gottman, J. (n.d.). Research FAQ. Retrieved from The Gottman Institute: https://www.gottman.com/about/research /faq/

Grover, S. (2016, November 10). How Does Poor Listening Affect Relationships? Retrieved from https://datingtips.match.com/poor-listening-affect-relationships-13443422.html

Hammond, C. (2017, October 12). The Importance of Dating Your Spouse. Retrieved from https://pro.psychcentral.com/exhausted-woman/2016/04/the-importance-of-dating-your-spouse/

Handel, S. (2019, January 22). The "Silent Treatment" Is A Sign of a Toxic Relationship. Retrieved from https://www.theemotionmachine.com/the-silent-treatment-is-a-sign-of-a-toxic-relationship/

Hardwick, C. (2017, January 5). 10 Reasons You Should Say "I Love You". Retrieved from https://www.bolde.com/10-reasons-say-love/

Hertenstein, M. J., Holmes, R., McCullough, M., & Keltner, D. (2009). The communication of emotion via touch. American Psychological Association, 566–573.

How to Stop Comparing your Partner with Others. (2019, February 1). Retrieved from https://www.betterlyf.com/articles/relationships/how-to-stop-comparing-your-partner-with-others/

Koole, S. L. (2013). Touch May Alleviate Existential Fears for People With Low Self-Esteem. Association for Psychological Science.

Light, K. C., Grewen, K. M., & Amico, J. A. (2005). More frequent partner hugs and higher oxytocin levels are linked to lower blood pressure and heart rate in premenopausal women. Biological Psychology, 5-21.

Manning-Schaffel, V. (2018, October 25). The health benefits of hugging. Retrieved from https://www.nbcnews.com/better/pop-culture/health-benefits-hugging-ncna920751

Murphy, M. L., Janicki-Deverts, D., & Cohen , S. (2018). Receiving a hug is associated with the attenuation of negative mood that occurs on days with interpersonal conflict. PloS One.

Ngo, S. (2018, June 4). Signs That Your Relationship's Honeymoon Phase Is Officially Over. Retrieved from https://www.cheatsheet.com/health-fitness/signs-the-honeymoon-phase-is-over.html/

Papp, L. M., Cummings, E. M., & Kouros, C. D. (2009). Demand-Withdraw Patterns in Marital Conflict in the Home. Personal Relationships, 285–300.

Raab, D. (2017, August 9). Deep Listening in Personal Relationships. Retrieved from https://www.psychologytoday.com/intl/blog/the-empowerment-diary/201708/deep-listening-in-personal-relationships

SarHarnis. (2020, March 2). 15 signs your spouse takes you for granted and doesn't care. Retrieved from https://www.bonobology.com/signs-spouse-takes-granted/

Schrodt, P., Witt, P. L., & Shimkowski, J. R. (2014). A Meta-Analytical Review of the Demand/Withdraw Pattern of Interaction and its Associations with Individual, Relational, and Communicative Outcomes. Communication Monographs, 28-58.

Sinrich, J. (2019, February 13). Why Saying "I Love You" Is So Important in a Marriage. Retrieved from https://www.marthastewartweddings.com/651160/why-saying-i-love-you-important-in-marriage

Smith, S. (2019, January 4). Why Is Dating Important in a Relationship. Retrieved from https://www.marriage.com/advice/relationship/why-is-dating-important/

Swindell, A. (2020, February 7). Why Marriage Shouldn't End Your Dating Life. Retrieved from https://relevantmagazine.com/life5/why-marriage-shouldnt-end-your-dating-life/

Thomson-Deveaux, A. (2017, August 8). Inside the Secret Sex Lives of Twentysomething Married Women. Retrieved from Cosmopolitan:

https://www.cosmopolitan.com/sex-love/a10295440/survey-twentysomething-married-women-sex-lives/

Made in the USA
Monee, IL
01 September 2020